**Location of the Yosemite Valley
and the Surrounding Uplands**

HIKER'S GUIDE

TO THE HIGH SIERRA

YOSEMITE

The Valley and
Surrounding Uplands

SIXTH EDITION

Jeffrey P. Schaffer

WILDERNESS PRESS
BERKELEY

Copyright © 1969, 1971, 1974 by Wilderness Press
Copyright © 1985, 1989, 1996, 1999, 2003 by Jeffrey P. Schaffer

SIXTH EDITION March 2003

Cover design by Jaan Hitt
Book design by Archetype Typography
All photographs by the author
Topographic maps revised and updated by the author, based on
U.S. Geological Survey maps
Front cover photo: © 2003 Mist Trail to Vernal Falls, Liberty Cap
                              in background
Back cover photo: © 2003 fissures at Taft Point
Frontispiece photo: © 2003 Half Dome and Yosemite Valley,
                              viewed from Eagle Peak

Library of Congress Card Catalog Number 96–3216
International Standard Book Number 0–89997–319–1
Manufactured in the United States

Published by Wilderness Press
             1200 5th St.
             Berkeley, CA 94710-1306
             (800) 443-7227
             FAX (510) 558-1696

Write, call or fax for a free catalog
Check our website for updates and new titles from Wilderness
Press: www.wildernesspress.com

Library of Congress Cataloging-in-Publication Data

Schaffer, Jeffrey P.
    Yosemite : a complete guide to the valley and surrounding
  uplands, including descriptions of more than 150 miles of trails /
  Jeffrey P. Schaffer. — 6th ed.
       p.   cm. — (High Sierra hiking guide)
    Includes bibliographical references (p.   ) and index.
    ISBN 0–89997–319–1
    1. Hiking—California—Yosemite National Park—Guidebooks.
  2. Trails—California—Yosemite National Park—Guidebooks. 3.
  Natural history— California—Yosemite National Park—
  Guidebooks. 4. Yosemite National Park (Calif.)—Guidebooks.
  I. Title.   II. Series.

  GV199.42.C22Y6772   2003
  917.94'47045—dc20   96–3216

Table of Contents

BACKPACK HIKES

Acknowledgments

Almost all of this book is a condensed version of part of Schaffer's *Yosemite National Park* guidebook, and in the "Acknowledgments" of that book he lists people who aided him on that project.

READ THIS!

One element of the beauty, freedom and excitement of the wilderness is the presence of risks that do not confront us at home. When you hike, you assume those risks. The fact that a trail is described in this book is not a representation that it will be safe for *you.* Trails vary greatly in difficulty and in the degree of conditioning and agility one needs to enjoy them safely.

On some hikes, routes may have changed or conditions may have deteriorated since the descriptions were written. Trail conditions can change from day to day, owing to weather and other factors. A trail that is safe on a dry day, may be unsafe under adverse weather conditions. A trail considered easy to moderately difficult by a highly conditioned, agile, and properly equipped hiker, may be completely unsafe for someone else.

Minimize your risks by being knowledgeable, prepared and alert. There are many good books and public courses on the subject, as well as guided trips. Be aware of your own limitations and alert to the conditions that exist when and where you are hiking. If conditions are dangerous, or if you're not prepared to deal with them safely, choose a different hike! It's better to waste a drive than to be the subject of a mountain rescue.

These warnings are not intended to scare you off the trails. Millions of people hike safely every year. The risks you face can be safely met, but only when and if you exercise your own independent judgment and common sense.

Have a good time!

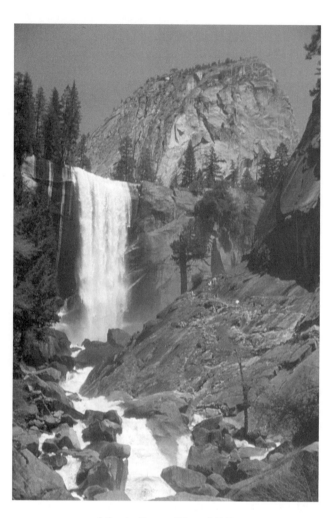

Liberty Cap and Vernal Fall

Introduction

FIRST PUBLISHED IN 1971, the Wilderness Press HIGH SIERRA HIKING GUIDES were the first *complete* guides for hiking and backpacking in the famous California High Sierra. There had long been a great demand for literature about America's favorite wilderness, John Muir's "Range of Light." To meet this demand, we undertook this guide series, which grew to 20 titles, each describing routes in a specific U.S. Geological Survey 15′ topographic quadrangle. Thirty years later, only three titles remained, and Wilderness Press is proud to continue these in our renamed HIKER'S GUIDE TO THE HIGH SIERRA series. These enduring classics are *the* source for information on many of California's favorite high country destinations in the Yosemite, Tuolumne Meadows, and Mt. Whitney areas.

Over this time span a few trail changes have occurred, and these are incorporated into the text as well as on the book's topographic map. As with all Wilderness Press titles, books in the HIKER'S GUIDE TO THE HIGH SIERRA series are based on first-hand observation and experience. There is absolutely no substitute for walking the trails, so the author has walked and mapped all the trails, in some cases several times over. Still, errors and out-of-date information can occur, so if you spot any, please contact us by email: *mail@wildernesspress.com.*

The purpose of each book in the series is threefold: first, to provide a reliable basis for planning a trip; second, to serve as a field guide while you are on the trail; and third, to stimulate you to further field investigation and background reading. In each guide there are a minimum of 100 described miles of trails, well above that in the *Tuolumne Meadows* guide.

In this short chapter we cover the basic logistics to hopefully make your visit to Yosemite Valley a pleasant one.

About two thirds of the trail descriptions in this hiking guide deal with trails in and about Yosemite Valley. Called

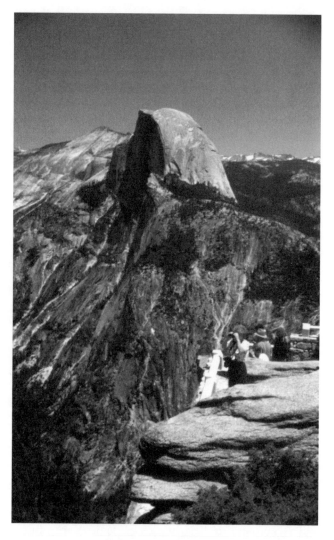

Half Dome from Glacier Point

"The Incomparable Valley," this is a magnet that attracts visitors from all over the world. As John Muir noted in the 1870s, the Sierra has several "Yosemites," though none of them matches Yosemite Valley in grandeur. Hetch Hetchy, to the north, is the foremost example of such a

"Yosemite." Though some of these "Yosemites" rival or exceed Yosemite Valley in their depth or the steepness of their walls, none has the prize-winning combination of its wide, spacious floor, its world-famous waterfalls, and its unforgettable monoliths—El Capitan and Half Dome.

The rest of the trail descriptions deal with trails in a rather undramatic part of the range. However, these descriptions do include a network of trails through a grove of giant sequoias; no such trail system exists at the Park's two other groves. Although thousands of persons visit this area's Mariposa Grove each day during the summer, the vast majority ride the trams. The few who explore the grove on foot are richly rewarded.

The area covered in this guide does not have enough lodges, hotels, and campgrounds to handle the millions of annual visitors, so make reservations well in advance. For lodging in Yosemite Valley and at the Wawona Hotel, contact the Yosemite Concession Services (559-252-4848 or yosemitepark.com). You can reserve up to a year and one day in advance. On private land in the Wawona area are The Redwoods (209-375-6256) and Camp Chilnualna (209-375-6295), which offer "cottages" with up to four bedrooms. Just outside the Park, near the start of the Glacier Point Road, is Yosemite West (209-642-2211), which offers condos and cottages. To camp in Yosemite Valley, make reservations with the National Park Reservation System (1-800-436-7275 or reservations.nps.gov). You can reserve up to 5 months in advance. The Wawona Campground is on the reservation system from May through September, but on a first-come, first-served basis the rest of the year. Bridalveil Campground, open in the summer season, is solely on a first-come, first-served basis. Finally, just below the Park's southern border is the USFS Summerdale Campground. South of it the Highway 41 towns of Fish Camp and Oakhurst offer additional lodging.

The History

"THE GRANDEUR OF THE SCENE was but softened by the haze that hung over the valley—light as gossamer—and by the clouds which partially dimmed the higher cliffs and mountains. This obscurity of vision but increased the awe with which I beheld it, and as I looked, a peculiar exalted sensation seemed to fill my whole being, and I found my eyes in tears with emotion." So wrote Dr. Lafayette Bunnell, a member of the Mariposa Battalion, of his group's discovery of Yosemite Valley on March 27, 1851. Today, many visitors seeing the Valley for the first time are struck with similar emotions.

The battalion entered the Valley in pursuit of a band of Ahwahnechee Indians under the leadership of Chief Teneiya. The band was captured, later released, and then decimated in 1853 by a band of Mono Indians. The Valley was now safe for tourists. James Hutchings was one of the earliest ones, and through his *Illustrated California Magazine* and his guidebooks the Valley became widely known. Roads, trails and hotels were built, guidebooks were written, and tourism increased. One important tourist was Frederick Law Olmsted, who visited the Valley and the Mariposa Grove of Big Trees in 1863 and noted that both were being ruined by commercial interests. He convinced U.S. Senator John Conness of California to introduce a park bill, which was subsequently signed by President Abraham Lincoln on June 30, 1864. The bill deeded the Valley and the Grove to California "for public use, resort and recreation."

But the lands surrounding these two tracts didn't fare well. Meadows were overgrazed by sheep (and to a lesser extent by cattle), and forests were ravaged by loggers. This habitat destruction was noted by a young Scotsman, John Muir, who first visited Yosemite Valley in 1868. Over the years he explored much of the High Sierra and criticized its exploitation, but his protestations fell on deaf ears until 1889, when he met Robert Underwood Johnson.

This editor of the very influential *Century Magazine* was impressed with both Muir and the High Sierra, and he had Muir write some Yosemite articles for his magazine. A park bill was introduced in Congress, and in October 1890, Yosemite National Park was created.

The bill, however, failed to stipulate how the Park should be administered. This task was given to the Army's Fourth Cavalry, which was stationed in Wawona. They stayed until the passage of the National Park Act of 1916, which established an administrative system for all the country's national parks and monuments. When the cavalry left Yosemite, they left behind an impressive record. They had driven sheep and cattle from the Park, had helped to settle property disputes, had laid the foundation for today's trail system, had mapped the Park in substantial detail, and had even planted trout in the Park's lakes. For Yosemite, the cavalry had by and large "come to the rescue."

One serious incursion the cavalry was unable to prevent was the creation of Hetch Hetchy Reservoir, which lies about 15 miles northwest of Yosemite Valley. John Muir and his fledgling Sierra Club had fought a losing battle to defeat this San Francisco water project. To build a massive dam required lots of timber scaffolding, and 6+ million board feet of timber were logged *inside the Park* by the Yosemite Lumber Company. More than 0.5 billion board feet of prime forest, including some of the Sierra's finest stands of sugar pines, were cut before 1930, when John D. Rockefeller, Jr. and the U.S. Government split the cost of buying up the logging company's interests. Today hikers can view part of the logged land—and walk along the abandoned railroad tracks—on Backpack Hike 2.

After World War II the Park's use greatly increased, and most of that use was confined to a small part of the Park—Yosemite Valley. The Valley was being loved to death. Beginning in 1970, the Park Service took steps to reduce the human impact in the Valley by instigating a shuttle-bus system, by reducing the number of campers and lodgers, by moving facilities and personnel outside the Valley, and by building bicycle paths. In the late 1990s, plans were underway to remove most of the vehicles from most of the valley, but actual implementation seems slow in coming. The decades-long goal of completely banning private vehicles from the Valley hopefully will be attained early in the 21st century.

View of El Capitan, Cathedral Rocks, and Bridalveil Falls from Valley View

The Geology

NO OTHER LOCALE in the Sierra Nevada receives so much use as does Yosemite Valley, this hiking guide's prime attraction. This has caused tremendous crowding, which in turn has led to ongoing controversy over solutions to reduce it. Likewise, the geomorphic history of the Valley —how it came to be formed—has been steeped in controversy. It began with Josiah D. Whitney, the first director of California's State Geological Survey, who proclaimed in 1865 that Yosemite Valley had been formed by downfaulting, which "explained" the angularity and verticality of its walls. Starting in 1869, John Muir explored the Yosemite area, and after several years of Sierran glacial explorations he wrote seven "Studies in the Sierra." Not only had glaciers entirely carved every canyon in the range, he trumpeted, but they had advanced west to the Pacific Ocean.

Not surprisingly, geologists did not accept all his findings, although over time they gravitated toward a combination of stream erosion and glacial erosion, rather than down-faulting, to explain the Valley's origin. Ironically, only James Hutchings came close to understanding how the Valley had been formed. Having lived in the Valley long enough to observe processes in action, he stood alone in recognizing the importance of mass wasting, stream erosion, flooding and former glacial erosion. He was more correct than was any geologist who followed him, but he lacked the academic credentials to be taken seriously by geologists.

To settle the Valley's origin "for all time," the U.S. Geological Survey in 1913 assigned François Matthes (pronounced "Mat'-tees") the task of explaining Yosemite Valley. All his findings would be accepted as the "Bible truth," and when his Professional Paper 160 finally appeared in 1930, it was heralded as a classic. Matthes' methodology for determining the amount of glacial erosion then was applied to glaciated ranges around the world. Unfortunately, until I began a serious investigation in the 1990s, no one had realized that his work was a fabrication. His diary indicates that he was torn between pleasing his professor, who incorrectly explained how glaciers transform landscapes, and the actual, contradictory field evidence. Ultimately, Matthes chose loyalty, wrote logical arguments, and precisely mapped glacial deposits that existed only in his mind. One easily visited area of his myriad deposits lies along the Four Mile Trail (Day Hike 17) at about elevation 5,150 feet. He mapped young morainal material below this elevation and old morainal material above it—but only bedrock and talus exist.

One reason why Matthes' work and its slight amendments by Clyde Wahrhaftig and N. King Huber have appeared so reasonable is that most experts have thought that major uplift of the range occurred mostly during the last few million years. If this view were correct, then erosion by both rivers and glaciers must have gone on at enormous rates to create such deep canyons in so short a geologic time. This myth of "late Cenozoic uplift" originated at least as early as the 1840s, and it would have been reinforced by the 1872 Owens Valley earthquake near Lone Pine, which created a 23-foot-high scarp. Everyone assumed that the range rose by this amount; no one asked if Owens Valley had subsided. Yet its bedrock floor, which lies beneath thousands of feet of sediments, is in places below sea level. It got below sea level not through river erosion but through down-faulting.

In 1898 the uplift myth received official sanction with the USGS publication of Leslie Ransome's Bulletin 89, which used a large lava flow, standing high above the floor of the Stanislaus River canyon, to quantify uplift. Ransome assumed that the lava had flowed down the granitic bedrock floor of a shallow, low-elevation canyon and in response to uplift the river cut down to its current level, creating a much deeper canyon. However, most of the 9-million-year-old lava flow lies atop earlier volcanic deposits, not atop granitic bedrock. In the vicinity of the Dardanelles, the base of the lava flow is 1,400 feet above a

rhyolite deposit that is at least 23 million years old. Therefore, the canyon was at least 1,400 feet deeper than Ransome had believed—perhaps much deeper, since most of
the earliest deposits have been eroded away. Ironically,
Ransome had mapped the volcanic deposits correctly; he
merely ignored the lower, older deposits that contradicted
his uplift hypothesis. Huber did the same in 1981 for the
San Joaquin River drainage and in 1990 for the Tuolumne
River drainage.

Fortunately, there are dozens of dated, mostly volcanic,
deposits in the Sierra Nevada, and their bases are in contact with the topography they buried. Therefore, one can
recreate that former topography and see how it compares
with today's topography. By doing this in my comprehen-
sive book, *The Geomorphic Evolution of the Yosemite Valley
and Sierra Nevada Landscapes* (see Recommended Reading), I was able to show that over the last 15 million years
of essentially modern climate, during which time almost
all Sierran uplift supposedly has occurred, resistant ridges
and monoliths have been reduced only by about five feet!
Canyon bottoms have been eroded more: perhaps tens of
feet, certainly not thousands of feet. For example, the net
erosion over the last 50 million years in the South Yuba
River canyon near Malakoff Diggins is too minor to
measure. And some 20 million years ago the Clark Fork
Stanislaus River, like others, was buried under voluminous deposits. Fortunately, some still remain near the
headwaters. What they show is that the granitic landscape
back then was virtually identical to today's, including all
the glacial landforms—cirques, hanging tributaries, etc.
—that supposedly have been created over the last 2 million years of major, episodic glaciation. Additionally,
these deep, old canyons contradict the uplift myth: had
major uplift occurred, then the canyon floors initially
would have been thousands of feet below sea level.

So where does this leave us with Yosemite Valley? The
granitic rocks in which it has developed solidified as dis-
crete bodies—plutons—beneath the earth's surface from
114 to 86 million years ago. According to a small but

growing number of geologists (from USGS, Cal Tech, and elsewhere), the upper few miles of the Sierran crust delaminated about 80 million years ago, "instantly" exposing the plutons. From about then to about 33 million years ago, tropical weathering and erosional processes created the range's landscapes, including Yosemite Valley, which took on a steep-walled, broad-floored aspect early on.

By the advent of modern climates 33 million years ago, you would have recognized the Valley. It would have been close to its present depth and about three-fourths its present width. Immediately before the first glaciation, about 2 million years ago, if not considerably earlier, the Valley looked very much as it does today. Minor widening occurred through retreat parallel to existing surfaces, not to steepening of slopes. My estimate of average wall retreat during this time is less than 500 feet, most of it due to rockfall rather than to glacial erosion. However, retreat of thick glaciers reduced pressure against the lower slopes, and this pressure release apparently induced rockfall, so glaciers indirectly widened Yosemite Valley, albeit minimally, despite glaciers entering the Valley perhaps some 50+ times. The earliest glaciers excavated some of fractured, tropically weathered bedrock lying beneath the Valley's broad floor, replacing it over time with glacial and stream sediments. The last glacier entered about 30,000 years ago, advanced through the Valley and into the Merced Gorge, then began to retreat about 18,000 years ago, leaving the Valley about 16,000 years ago. Supposedly the Valley then was occupied by a deep lake—another geo-myth, dating back at least to Whitney. This guide's trail descriptions have elaborations on this brief discourse, and they identify evidence you can examine for yourself.

The Biology

YOU CANNOT FORGET your first visit to Yosemite: the enormous granite monoliths of El Capitan, the Cathedral Rocks and Half Dome, the leaping, tumultuous waterfalls, the glacially smoothed domes of Tuolumne Meadows, the pristine lakes and snow-clad high peaks. Of these features only the waterfalls move, and none are living. For most visitors, memories of living forms—except for giant sequoias—are likely to take a back seat to the inanimate landscape, although many out-of-state visitors will be duly impressed with the size of some conifers besides the sequoias. But despite the seemingly barren summits and cliffs, Yosemite is predominantly a landscape of forest green. Along most of this guide's trails, conifers shade the way.

The largest conifer in the area is the giant sequoia, which is the uncontested holder of the world heavyweight crown. Its ancestors go back to the days of the dinosaurs, but we don't know where it originated or when it migrated westward into the Sierra Nevada. The trees would have entered it no later than about 33 million years ago, if not by before 65 million years ago. The tree's size hasn't always assured it success. First, it is adapted to gentle-to-moderate slopes possessing sufficient soil moisture to endure the dry summers. Before glaciation, such slopes were far more abundant, but glaciers removed soil and underlying, decomposed bedrock, condemning the species to the lower and southern unglaciated parts of its range. Second, its seeds are not eaten and transported by migrating birds, hence some suitable slopes are not colonized. And third, for its seeds to produce viable seedlings, the tree needs cone-boring cerambycid beetles, seed-eating Douglas' squirrels (chickarees), and periodic fires. Remove any of these, and a sequoia grove is in peril. (For more sequoia natural history, see **Day Hike 25**).

Fire, which is essential for sequoias, also is important for many sun-loving plants—and the animals that

Top photo: cones of ponderosa pine (top), Douglas-fir (right), and sugar pine (bottom). Bottom photo: cones of western white pine (left) and red fir (right).

White-fir branches (top photo) versus red-fir branches
(bottom photo).

depend on them. In this guide's area, much of the forest has been burned since a major fire in 1974. After a forest fire, wildflowers and shrubs greatly increase their numbers. Over time, they may be succeeded by oaks, which shade them out at lower elevations, while pines and incense-cedars do so higher up. Possibly firs may come to dominate the forest, if abundant soil moisture is present. If fires occur fairly regularly—every decade or two—litter accumulation will be minor and only ground fires will result, eliminating brush and young trees. If fires do not occur for many decades, litter accumulation will be major and a crown fire will result, destroying a forest and allowing the process of plant succession to begin once again.

A sequoia grove is a relatively restricted plant community, which, like the area's other plant communities, includes animals and microorganisms as well as plants. As in that community, the plants, animals, and microorganisms in other communities are regulated in number largely by their mutual interactions and by nonbiotic influences such as soil, slope, and microclimate. If you drive from Arch Rock Entrance Station up to Yosemite Valley and then up the Glacier Point Road to the Mono Meadow trailhead (**Backpack Hike 4**), you'll pass through several plant communities.

From the entrance station you'll drive mostly through a canyon live (gold-cup) oak woodland, although shrubs such as Mariposa manzanitas dominate dry spots, as at the foot of El Capitan. Walking through the woodland, you'll find it seemingly devoid of animals, save perhaps for raucous Steller's jays or acorn and pileated woodpeckers. But the animals are there. The oak's roots are tapped by root fungi, which are grazed by flat bugs and carrion beetles, which are eaten by western skinks (lizards), which are preyed upon by gopher snakes, which are seized by mountain king snakes, which are carried off by red-tailed hawks. And there are hundreds more interacting species. Incidentally, among this vegetation, where ground rodents abound, so do rattlesnakes.

As you drive on toward Bridalveil Fall, you'll pass through a mixed-conifer forest, dominated by ponderosa pine, incense-cedar (not a true cedar), white fir, and Douglas-fir (not a true fir). Black oaks have replaced live oaks and, correspondingly, western gray squirrels have replaced California ground squirrels.

The shady forest is a stark contrast to Yosemite Valley's meadows, which, like the large one at Wawona, have been greatly altered from their natural state. Early Valley residents lowered the water table to drain bogs, which led to meadow invasion by trees. Introduced livestock grazed heavily on the native meadow plants, though these plants were most affected by the usually unintentional introduction of alien plants. Galen Clark noted that in the 30 years that had passed since the Valley had been given "protection," its luxuriant native grasses and wildflowers had decreased to only one-fourth of their original number.

From the Valley you'll drive west up to lower, open slopes of Turtleback Dome, then head south across formerly burned slopes up to a junction with the Glacier Point Road. Along this leg are local areas of dense shrubs —mostly ceanothus—as well as forest areas that have sugar pines, which were extensively logged before 1930.

On the Glacier Point Road you'll climb east, again across formerly burned slopes, entering a red-fir forest before arriving at Badger Pass. This is replaced by a lodgepole-pine forest in the flat of the Bridalveil Campground area. This rather sudden change in tree type is due to the flat's high water table; the lodgepoles embrace it, the red firs abhor it.

Where the road bends north, you'll reach the Mono Meadow Trail, which begins in a grove of mature red firs. Where these trees are not burned, the forest floor is very shady, so few plants grow on it. Some that do, such as the snow plant, derive part of their nourishment by tapping their roots into soil fungi. The forest has a solemn, cathedral-like feeling, for the trees are lofty and silence usually prevails. With little plant life on the forest floor, there is an absence of scolding rodents and singing birds.

If you were to take the Mono Meadow Trail east to the Buena Vista Trail and follow it south, you'd climb into other communities, and also would see more evidence of past fires. (Natural fires are an integral part of most ecosystems.) With elevation you'd note western white ("silver") pines, followed by snow-loving mountain hemlocks. The hemlocks, unfortunately, prolong the duration of snow cover, which is a nuisance to hikers but a boon to snow mosquitoes. These blood-suckers (the females, that is) may be annoying to you, but they are major pollinators of the area's wildflowers.

The Buena Vista Trail guides you to the Buena Vista Peak environs, which lie in the subalpine realm. Many plants up there are dwarfed, for winter's driving, sub-freezing winds are extreme, and plants survive better buried under snow than protruding above it. Near the top of 9,709-foot Buena Vista Peak—the highest summit in the area—stunted, gnarled whitebark pines grow in dense clusters. These attract Clark's nutcrackers, which are large, gray relatives of jays. The birds thrive on the pines' seeds, and they bury caches to last them through the year. The birds will eat most of the seeds, but a few survive to give rise to more pines. Thus the birds help to perpetuate the clusters of whitebark pines, just as the Douglas' squirrels, lower down, help to perpetuate the groves of giant sequoias.

That first impression of the Valley—
white water, azaleas, cool fir caverns,
tall pines and stolid oaks, cliffs rising
to undreamed-of heights, the poignant
sounds and smells of the Sierra . . .
was a culmination of experience so
intense as to be almost painful.

— Ansel Adams

The Trails

THIS GUIDEBOOK IS AIMED at hikers—day hikers in par-
ticular. The eastern half of Yosemite Valley also has bike
paths, which are mentioned where encountered. Bicyclists
share these with hikers, but horses are banned. Seasonally
(during the summer and then some), both horses and
bikes can be rented.

The hikes in this book are two kinds: day hikes and
backpack hikes. For the latter, you'll need a wilderness
permit, which you can get in person either at the Yosemite
Valley Wilderness Center, located near the Valley's Visitor
Center, or at the Wawona Ranger Station. Unfortunately,
backcountry overuse has made a quota system necessary.
Up to fifty percent of each trailhead quota may be re-
served in advance by mail, phone, or in person at the
Wilderness Center (209-372-0740 or nps.gov/yose/wil-
derness). The following information is needed to process
your reservation: name, address, phone number, number of people and stock (no pets!) in your party, entry
and exit dates, starting and ending trailheads, principal
destination, and all alternative trailheads and dates you
are willing to accept. Starting in the late 1990s the center
charged for permits, and in the early 2000s the fee had
increased to $5.00 per person. With permit in hand, you
can spend the night before your trek in the Backpackers Walk-In Campground, north of the Valley's horse
stables.

There are three advantages to day hiking. First, you
don't have to worry about the wilderness-permit hassle.
Second, you don't have to worry about protecting your
food overnight in backcountry bearproof boxes, or in
bulky, heavy, bear-resistant food canisters (which you can
rent for a few dollars). Bearbagging is discouraged by
the Park Service. Bears, incidentally, rarely molest hikers;
mostly they, like rodents, go after your food. Finally, you
don't need to boil, filter, or chemically treat pristine-
looking but possibly polluted backcountry water, for you

can carry a day's supply of water in your pack. Before hiking, familiarize yourself with advice, cautions, and regulations found in the quarterly newspaper, the *Yosemite Guide,* available at every entrance station.

Note that each hike in this book has a grade: a number-letter combination. The numbers refer to each hike's total mileage, as follows: 1=0–4.9 miles, 2=5.0–9.9 miles, 3=10.0–14.9 miles, 4=15.0–19.9 miles, and 5=20.0+ miles. The letters refer to total elevation gain: A=0–499 feet, B=500–999 feet, C=1,000–1,999 feet, D=2,000–3,999 feet, and E=4,000+ feet. The words easy, moderate, and strenuous describe a hike's difficulty for a person in good shape, given the recommended time. Of course, you can decrease the difficulty of most hikes by taking longer to do them.

At the end of each trailhead description is a **boldfaced** letter-number combination, which corresponds to the letter-number grid on the book's map where the hike starts. This is provided for those hikers not familiar with the trail system of this part of the Park.

In a year of normal precipitation, the trails are virtually snow-free from early July through early October, although down in Yosemite Valley and about Wawona, they are free from about early April through late November. When the trail is partly snowbound, you can usually still follow it with the aid of ducks or blazes. A duck is made up of two or more rocks, arranged in an obviously unnatural fashion. Ducks are often placed along a trail where it traverses bedrock. A blaze is a scar hewn in a trailside tree trunk, usually in the shape of an **i** or a **T**.

To see wildflowers at their prime (also prime mosquito time), visit the lower trails in May or June and the higher ones in July. If you plan to swim in a backcountry lake, in the Valley's Merced River, or in Wawona's South Fork Merced River, visit in late July or early August, when water temperature usually is at its maximum. Wawona's South Fork can be quite warm by mid-afternoon.

Of course, many people visit Yosemite to see its waterfalls, which usually are best from mid-May to mid-June.

Avoid, however, the Memorial Day weekend—and the
Fourth of July and Labor Day weekends—when the Park
becomes severely overcrowded. For relative solitude, visit
the Valley or Wawona from mid-September through November, when the summer crowds are gone and the skiers
have not yet arrived.

DAY HIKE 1
Valley Floor, West Loop

Distance: 6.9 miles loop trip

Grade: 2B, easy half-day hike

Trailhead: Bridalveil Fall parking lot, 120 yards before
the descending Wawona Road reaches a junction on
the floor of Yosemite Valley. **C1.**

This is the first of six Yosemite Valley floor hikes in this
book, which are arranged from west to east. On this first
loop hike you'll see Bridalveil Fall, the Cathedral Rocks,
and El Capitan all at close range.

You could start this loop from any of several pullouts
along the Valley's roads, but you're starting from the
Bridalveil Fall Parking lot, since it has the most parking
space. From the lot's east end you hike just two minutes
on a paved trail to a junction, veer right and parallel a
Bridalveil Creek tributary as you climb an equally short
trail up to its end. During May and June, when Bridalveil
Fall is at its best, the trail's-end viewpoint is drenched in
spray, making the last part of the trail very slippery and
making photography from this vantage point nearly
impossible. Early settlers named this fall for the filmy,
veil-like aspect it has in summer after its flow has greatly
diminished. However, their predecessors, the Miwok Indians, named it Pohono, the "fall of the puffing winds,"
for at low volume its water is pushed around by gusts of
wind.

After descending back to the trail junction and turning right, you quickly encounter several branches of

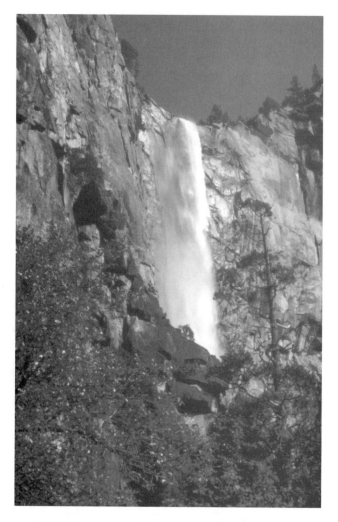

Bridalveil Fall or *Pohono*, the fall of the puffing winds

Bridalveil Creek, each churning along a course that cuts through old rockfall debris. From a junction with a short trail to the Valley's Southside Drive, you continue ahead on a broad trail—the old Wawona Road until 1933—and almost reach the present road, then quickly veer right to climb up to the crest of Bridalveil Moraine. From it you get a good view of the loose west wall of Lower Cathedral Rock and also of overhanging Leaning Tower.

Just past the moraine's crest you enter a gully lined with big-leaf maples, and here you have an excellent head-on view of mammoth El Capitan. Then, while only yards away from the base of the forbidding north face of Lower Cathedral Rock, you see a high, broad ledge, covered with canyon live oaks, that almost cuts the face in two. You continue east through a conifer forest, soon crossing a narrow, open, talus field. At its base stands a second moraine, similar to Bridalveil Moraine. Both were left about 16,000 years ago, when the last glacier, while receding, temporarily halted its retreat and dropped some of its load.

Walking among white firs, incense-cedars, ponderosa pines, Douglas-firs, and black oaks, you continue on a generally view-impaired route to a brief climb almost to the base of overwhelming Middle Cathedral Rock, and here you'll find it worth your effort to scramble 50 yards up to the actual base. Touching the base of this monolith's overpowering, 2,000-foot-high face can be a humbling experience. Next you traverse briefly beneath the massive northeast face and its two pinnacles, and then descend slightly to a level area, from which you could walk northwest a bit to a turnout on Southside Drive. From that turnout you can plainly see the Cathedral Spires. These spires, and the 500-foot-high buttress they stand on, resemble a two-towered Gothic cathedral—hence the name. Despite their apparent inaccessibility, both were first climbed way back in 1934, during the early days of Valley climbing. Now, each is harder to climb, since rockfall altered the original ascent routes.

About a 0.3-mile walk beyond the level area you arrive at a signed trail, veer left, northwest, on it, and descend to a point on the eastbound road only 20 yards west of the Cathedral Picnic Area entrance. Those few who head north to the picnic area are rewarded with two classic views, one of El Capitan and the other of the Three Brothers. The route, however, continues northwest almost to a

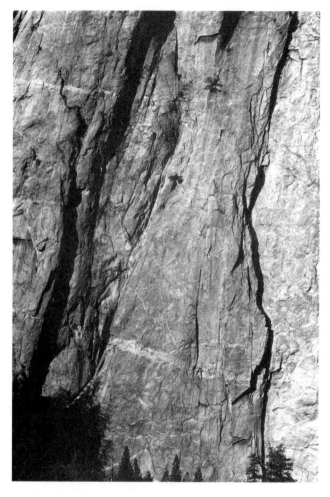

Lower north face of Middle Cathedral Rock

bend in the Merced River, from which you may see on summer days, sunbathers basking on the long, sandy beach of the far bank. Since the route eventually goes over to that vicinity, summertime hikers with swimsuits on can shortcut across the wide, chest-deep Merced to that beach. Non-swimmers follow the trail briefly west to the

El Capitan Bridge. Here, by the eastern edge of El Capitan Meadow, the hiker gets reflective views of the Cathedral Rocks, and one can see why the Miwok Indians visualized the lower rock as a giant acorn.

From the El Capitan Bridge you walk north either along the road or its adjacent riverbank trail to a sharp bend. By continuing east from there for about 250 yards you reach the site of Devils Elbow Picnic Area, closed in 1993 due to riverbank erosion from heavy use. However, above a second river bend there is access to the sandy beach.

From the first river bend you cross the main road and start west along an old road that in 0.3 mile comes to a small hollow from whose north end a climbers' trail ascends to the foot of El Capitan. This is a worthy excursion. The 3,000-foot route from the foot up its "Nose" takes less than one day for world-class climbers, and the first to ascend it without direct-aid slings was Lynn Hill. Rock climbing is a sport where women indeed are on par with men.

Beyond the hollow the road rolls gently west and then southwest to a trail branching west. You stick to the closed road and quickly reach the Valley's Northside Drive at the west end of El Capitan Meadow. After the Park was created in 1890 this meadow became the Valley's first campground and Bridalveil Meadow soon became the second. Three other free, meadow campgrounds soon followed, in contrast to the forested ones today. Back then, horse pasturage was the prime concern, hence the need for meadow sites.

Leaving the meadow's edge you walk briefly west along the paved road and cross two seasonal branches of Ribbon Creek. In 0.25 mile you come to a dirt road, and by walking just a few paces up it you immediately reach a westbound trail. After walking about five minutes west on it you cross a low recessional moraine, then drop almost to the paved road's edge. Here a turnout provides drivers and hikers with an unobstructed view of Bridalveil Fall.

Under the pleasant shade of ponderosa pines and incense-cedars you continue west, passing some cabin-size rockfall blocks immediately before skirting the north end of the Bridalveil Meadow moraine. Soon you enter a swampy area with cattails and at its west end cross trickling Black Spring. Past the spring the trail more or less parallels the westbound road, shortly arriving at the back side of the Valley View scenic turnout. Here you see El Capitan, Bridalveil Fall and the Cathedral Rocks magnificently rising high above the stately conifers that line Bridalveil Meadow. Barely rising above the trees are the distant landmarks of Clouds Rest, Half Dome, and Sentinel Rock.

Beyond Valley View the forested trail quickly reaches its westernmost point at Pohono Bridge. From a stream-gaging station across it your feet tread a riverside path past popular roadside Fern Spring, then past generally unknown trailside Moss Spring. Mountain (Pacific) dogwoods add springtime beauty as sunlight filters down to light up their translucent leaves and their large, petal-like, creamy-white bracts. Douglas-firs locally dominate as you hike to Bridalveil Meadow. Here you walk northeast along the eastbound road's side, staying above a seasonally boggy meadow. By the far edge the trail resumes, and goes north to a bend to cross the Bridalveil Meadow moraine. Previously this has been called the terminal moraine of the last glacier, but that one actually advanced about five miles farther, down into the lower part of Merced Gorge. Forty yards north of the bend is a plaque on a large rock, dedicated to Dr. Lafayette Bunnell, who was in the Valley's 1851 discovery party.

From the moraine you parallel the Merced River southeast almost to the eastbound road, which you can take 0.2 mile east to the Wawona Road, then go briefly up it to the Bridalveil Fall parking lot. Doing so in springtime avoids the possibility of getting wet feet in the nearby fords of multibranched Bridalveil Creek. After the last creek crossing the trail parallels the creek's northern branch east about 300 yards to long turnouts on both sides of the eastbound road. Here you can head southwest on the road to the parking lot or from the turnout on the far side of the road find a short trail going southeast to the trail you originally started on. On it retrace your steps 0.3 mile southwest to the lot.

DAY HIKE 2
Valley Floor, Yosemite Lodge Loop

Distance: 7.0 miles loop trip

Grade: 2A, easy half-day hike

Trailhead: Yosemite Falls parking lot, which is just west of the Yosemite Creek bridge. If full, try parking just south, in the Yosemite Lodge. Better yet, take the shuttle bus to the lot. **D1.**

Most of this loop is relatively quiet and lightly traveled. On it you'll get a classic view of the Three Brothers plus other less famous but equally dramatic views.

Behind the restrooms at the west end of the Yosemite Falls parking lot you'll find a trail heading southwest. On it you almost touch the main road, then curve right to the base of Swan Slab, which is a low cliff that attracts many climbers. A little less than 0.5 mile from the falls' lot you reach the Yosemite Falls trail (**Day Hike 10**), then pass above Camp 4 (Sunnyside) Walk-In Campground, a no-reservation campground heavily patronized by climbers. The trail next descends south along the campground's west edge, then parallels the Valley's westbound road 0.25 mile before crossing it.

On another trail segment you parallel the road southwest, and in about a minute you may see a trail, branching southeast. This use trail goes across the west edge of grassy Leidig Meadow to a sandy beach beside the Merced River. From the west edge of the meadow you get one of the Valley's best views, which includes North Dome, Royal Arches, Washington Column, Clouds Rest, and Half Dome. Partly obscuring Half Dome is a large descending

**Ranger Rock, and Middle and Lower Brothers
from picnic area east of Devils Elbow**

ridge on whose dry slopes the Four Mile Trail (**Day Hike 17**) zigzags down from Glacier Point. Looking west from Leidig Meadow, you see the Three Brothers, named for three sons of Chief Teneiya who were taken prisoner here in May 1851 by the Mariposa Battalion. The vertical east face of Middle Brother was the origin of a March 1987 rockfall that left most of the rocky debris you are about to cross. Shrubs and young trees are invading the debris slopes—talus—but a future rockfall could eradicate them.

From the trail junction the main trail quickly is sandwiched between the westbound road above and the silent river below. Light-colored, giant boulders from recent rockfalls contrast with darker, lichen-covered ones of much older rockfalls. Soon you leave the river's side and parallel the road at a short distance, hiking through a forest of pine, incense-cedar, and oak. After a mile of walking along the trail, part with fair views, you arrive at the El Capitan Picnic Area site, closed due to riverbank erosion from overuse (now no river access). A trail north-northeast goes to Northside Drive and the new El Capitan Picnic Area. In 0.3 mile you enter a meadow and have views of many of the Valley's features, particularly El Capitan, the Three Brothers, and the Cathedral Rocks. In the past the path split in the meadow, the two branches then rejoining in about 0.1 mile at the roadside site of the Devil Elbow Picnic Area, also closed due to overuse. However, there still is access to its sandy beach.

From the picnic area site the trail quickly curves south, hugging both road and fenced-off river for 0.25 mile to the El Capitan Bridge—one of the Valley's most scenic spots (see **Day Hike 1**), where again there is river access. At the bridge's east end the trail resumes, heads east to a bank opposite the south end of the Devils Elbow beach, then angles southeast to Southside Drive. Just 20 yards east lies the entrance to the Cathedral Picnic Area and on its road you walk north down to the riverbank for two famous and instructive views. Look northeast and note the similarity among the Three Brothers. They present a classic case of joint-controlled topography. Each is bounded on the east and south by nearly vertical joint planes and on the west by an oblique-angle joint plane. These three planes govern the shape of each brother. Now look northwest and see the massive south face of El Capitan and on

View from Leidig Meadow of North Dome, Royal Arches, Washington Column, below Clouds Rest, and Half Dome

the east part of it identify the dark-gray "North America map," which is a band of diorite that intruded and then solidified within the slightly older El Capitan granite.

Leaving the willow-lined Merced, you return to the trail, cross the road, and walk 250 yards southeast to a junction with the Valley's south-side trail. On it you start east and immediately cross a creek bed that is lined with youthful ponderosa pines which sprang up after a flood. Upstream you see overhanging Taft Point, then see it again as you progress east. After 0.5 mile of shady, south-side walking, you come to a huge, trailside slab, on whose flat summit are about 20 mortar holes made by the Indians to grind acorns to flour. Not a glacier-transported rock, this 1,000-ton slab broke off a steep wall of the obvious side canyon above you. As you continue on, Douglas-firs and white firs mingle with the more dominant ponderosa pines, incense-cedars, and black oaks.

You have scattered views over the next mile, which takes you to Sentinel Creek—usually reduced to just a trickle by the first day of summer. After the summer solstice you're lucky if multistage Sentinel Fall, located high in the creek's canyon, is even a gossamer mist. Voluminous only in flood stage, this fall is best seen in the warming days of late May.

After crossing the creek you come to an old spur road—the end of the Four Mile Trail from Glacier Point (**Day Hike 17**). In this vicinity once stood Leidig's Hotel, the westernmost of several pioneer hotels. Beyond here the trail soon draws close to the Valley's eastbound road, and where you see a large parking area, about 0.25 mile beyond the old spur road, you leave the trail, cross the eastbound road, and enter a picnic area. Black's Hotel once stood in this area, together with Galen Clark's cabin. Clark was one of the Valley's first tourists, and later became Yosemite's first guardian.

Descending through the picnic area you reach a long, sturdy bridge that replaces a much earlier suspension bridge across the Merced River. It provides good views of Yosemite Falls, Royal Arches, Washington Column, North Dome, Clouds Rest, Sentinel Rock, the Cathedral Rocks, and the Three Brothers. From its far end you take a broad, paved foot-and-bike path north to a bend in the road on the grounds of Yosemite Lodge. The path next winds northeast, then heads north, finally crossing the Valley's Northside Drive on the east side of the entrance to the lodge's grounds. This spot is also the west entrance to the Yosemite Falls parking lot, your starting point.

**The clearest way into the universe
is through a forest wilderness.**

— John Muir

DAY HIKE 3
Valley Floor, Yosemite Village Loop

Distance: 3.3 miles loop trip

Grade: 1A, easy 2-hour hike

Trailhead: Same as for Day Hike 2. **D1.**

Famous views of Yosemite Falls, Half Dome, and Royal Arches are seen along this short hike.

Avoiding hordes of visitors going north to the Lower Yosemite Fall bridge, you start from the parking lot's east end and walk southeast, quickly bridge Yosemite Creek, then cross the main road to start east on a trail along its south side. The trail quickly branches, and you angle right, away from the road to immediately cross a short spur road south. Beyond it a paved foot-and-bike path enters a beautiful, view-packed meadow, through which you start southeast but have the option to branch right, bridge the Merced River, and head toward the Yosemite chapel.

By not branching right in the meadow, you end at a parking area with picnic tables, just north of a 1994-vintage Sentinel Bridge, built immediately above the site of its predecessor. Often during August, when Upper Yosemite Fall is only a vestige of its springtime self, rafters with life vests slowly float down the river, adding a human element to the famous tree-framed view of stately Half Dome. By strategically locating their hotel in the area between this bridge and the chapel, Buck Beardsley and G. Hite in 1859 provided guests with the best of all possible views. Business, however, was poor, and in 1864 James Hutchings—one of the Valley's first tourists—bought the hotel.

From the south end of Sentinel Bridge you walk east on a riverbank trail, then cross the adjacent one-way road. Now you continue east beside the road, pass the seasonally bustling Housekeeping Camp, and soon arrive at the granite-stone LeConte Memorial Lodge. It is named for

Sentinel Rock from Sentinel Bridge

Joseph LeConte, who was the first geology professor at Berkeley's then-infant University of California. During the summer of 1870 he visited Yosemite Valley, met John Muir, and was profoundly impressed by both.

Leaving the lodge, its trailside Indian mortar holes, and its large boulders chalked by climbers, you cross the road and follow a short path north along the east side of the Housekeeping Camp, reaching a bridge to the site of flooded, closed Lower Riverside Campground. Heading toward Yosemite Falls, you leave behind views of Glacier Point, Glacier Point Apron, and Grizzly Peak as you follow a path downstream alongside alders and willows. On this short stretch large blocks were laid along the bank to prevent the river from meandering into either camp. All told, the river was once lined with about 14,500 feet of rip-rap revetment. Ponderosa pines, incense-cedars, and black oaks shade you to a small stretch of Ahwahnee Meadow that you cross just before the Valley's central road. In it the foot-and-bike path momentarily heads straight toward Upper Yosemite Fall. Here you have clear views east of North Dome, Royal Arches, Washington Column, and Half Dome. Below these towering landmarks stands one of America's grandest hotels, the Ahwahnee, opened in 1927.

After you cross the central road you walk north, shaded by large black oaks growing along the west edge of Ahwahnee Meadow. In 0.25 mile you reach the west end of the Church Bowl, which has a paved roadside path, and just behind it, a dirt one, which you ascend northwest into canyon live oaks. Climbing from the Church Bowl up past the Valley's medical clinic, you quickly reach Indian Canyon Creek. Its canyon was a principal Valley exit used by the Indians heading up to the north rim, and early pioneers built a trail of sorts up to it, then west to a Yosemite Falls overlook. In early season you may note one of the Valley's lesser-known falls, Lehamite Falls, which plunges down a branch of Indian Canyon.

Beyond the canyon's creek and its huge rockfall boulders (the Valley has widened more from rockfall than from glacial erosion), you climb northwest to avoid Park buildings and residences, then contour west beneath sky-piercing Arrowhead Spire and the highly fractured Castle Cliffs. Approaching a spur trail down to nearby government stables, you spy Lost Arrow—a giant pinnacle high on the wall of Upper Yosemite Fall. Heading west 0.25 mile toward Lower Yosemite Fall, you come to a junction. From it a trail descends along Yosemite Creek to the trailhead, but you continue 0.25 mile west to reach the highly visited bridge near the base of Lower Yosemite Fall. Along this last stretch a sawmill once stood, its large blade powered by the creek's water. John Muir built this sawmill for James Hutchings "to cut lumber for cottages . . . from the fallen pines which had been blown down in a violent windstorm [winter of 1867–68]."

From the bridge May and June visitors are treated to the thunderous roar and copious spray of the lower fall, but by late August the fall is usually reduced to a mist, and in some years it dries entirely by September. Dry or not, the fall should not be examined at close range, for even if boulder-choked Yosemite Creek is bone-dry, its rocks are water-polished and very slippery. Before leaving the bridge, note how the lower fall has indirectly cut its al-cove. Stream erosion has barely cut into the granitic bedrock since the last glacier disappeared about 16,000 years ago, but in winter the fall's spray freezes in the surrounding rocks, expands, and pries loose lower slabs that in turn remove support from the upper ones. The resulting myriad rockfall boulders then over time are rounded by stream action. These boulders, being locally derived, offer a gauge with which to estimate the amount of postglacial alcove rockfall. Walking back to the parking-lot trailhead, stop many times to get views of both Upper and Lower Yosemite Falls. Long ago a swath of trees was logged just to provide these views.

DAY HIKE 4
Valley Floor, Camp Curry Loop

Distance: 2.8 miles loop trip

Grade: 1A, easy 2-hour hike

Trailhead: Camp Curry parking lot, in eastern Yosemite Valley. **D1.**

More like a stroll, this is the easiest hike described in this guide. It is recommended for those who enjoy a leisurely pace, who want to take time to commune with squirrels, birds, and wildflowers, and who want to reflect on the Valley's natural and human history.

Back in the 1860s, long before a car entered the Valley, what is now the Camp Curry parking lot was an apple orchard, and rows of these fruit trees still grow in it today. From the lot's southeast corner you follow a paved path east along the south edge of a paved road. Both soon bend southeast and equally soon reach a junction with a shuttle-bus road to Happy Isles. Seventy yards beyond the junction the path crosses a short spur road to a trailhead parking lot for wilderness-permit holders only (e.g., **Backpack Hike 1**). This lot was a former garbage dump, which attracted bears, which were fed by rangers until

A tagged black bear on a tree limb

1941—the start of the bear problem. As backpackers became far more numerous in the 1960s, "delinquent" Yosemite bears who were kicked out of the Valley pursued them into new territory and eventually over much of the High Sierra. From this lot you can also hike up to the base of broad, curving Glacier Point Apron, a good place to view climbers. "Sticky soled" shoes, developed in the 1980s, allowed climbers to waltz up new routes that would have been unthinkable in the '70s.

You could take the paved, roadside path to Happy Isles, but a quieter one begins from the southeast edge of the trailhead parking lot. This rolls southeast, staying about 100–150 yards from the unseen shuttle-bus road. In 0.3 mile it intersects a southbound stock trail that links the Valley stables to the John Muir Trail. Beyond this intersection you head east on planks across a boggy area, and although mosquitoes may be bothersome in late spring and early summer, the bog then produces its best wildflowers. At a huge, lone boulder by the bog's east side, the trail angles southeast toward the hub of the Happy Isles area.

You'll probably see dozens if not hundreds of visitors in this area, and here you'll find, besides restrooms near the shuttle-bus road, an informative nature center. A July 1996 rockfall from the top of a cliff to the southwest stopped just short of the center, as you can see from the debris. While here, visit adjacent Happy Isles.

Departing north from Happy Isles, you have a choice of three pleasant routes: the Merced's west-bank trail, its east-bank trail, and the shuttle-bus road's east-side trail. The east-side trail begins about 100 yards south of the road's bridge, where it branches right, away from the east-bank trail. On the east-side trail you pass some cabin-size, moss-and-lichen-covered rockfall blocks, and then, where the trail climbs to cross the "Medial Moraine" (actually a recessional end moraine left by the Merced River glacier), you leave the trail to descend momentarily west to cross the road to the west-bending river. Both riverbank trails are relaxing strolls along the azalea-lined river, but perhaps the east-bank trail is more interesting since it traverses along the base of the west-trending moraine.

Skirting the base, the east-bank trail goes northwest almost to the Valley stables. There, at the moraine's end, turn left and immediately cross Clarks Bridge, named for Galen Clark, the Park's first guardian. From its west side, west-bank-trail hikers now join you for a brief walk past the entrances to the Upper and Lower Pines campgrounds. Beyond them you soon meet the southeast-heading shuttle-bus road, cross it, and walk west along a roadside trail leading past the north edge of the parking-lot trailhead.

DAY HIKE 5
Valley Stables to Mirror Lake

Distance: 3.3 miles loop trip

Grade: IA, easy 2-hour hike

Trailhead: Walk or take the shuttle bus through the Pines campgrounds to a shuttle-bus stop just across Clarks Bridge, and near a parking lot for patrons of the Yosemite stables. **D1.**

First cars and then shuttle buses once went to Mirror Lake and Indian Caves, but now the road is used by bicyclists. Most hikers also use it, though paths offer quieter route to these sites.

The low ridge you see just behind the shuttle-bus stop is the Valley's "Medial Moraine," so named because early geologists thought it formed where the Tenaya Creek and Merced River glaciers merged. A trail goes east along each side of the moraine, the south-side, riverbank trail being more scenic and quieter. On it you walk east along the base of the moraine, then at a junction veer left to the adjacent shuttle-bus road. Immediately before this junction is a large white rock derived from the upper Merced River drainage, indicating that its receding glacier left this end moraine.

You cross the road and ascend a spur trail about 40 yards east to a main trail. Starting north on it you immediately top the moraine's crest, then descend northwest toward a road junction. The shuttle-bus road goes west to the starting point while bicyclists bound for Mirror Lake take the road north. Still on the trail, you meander north, skirting an area of giant rockfall boulders that testify to the instability of Half Dome's west flank. Beyond them you come to a trail intersection beside Tenaya Bridge. West, the trail parallels Tenaya Creek to the back side of the stables. East, it dies out, for its upper part was not repaired after the January 1997 flood damage.

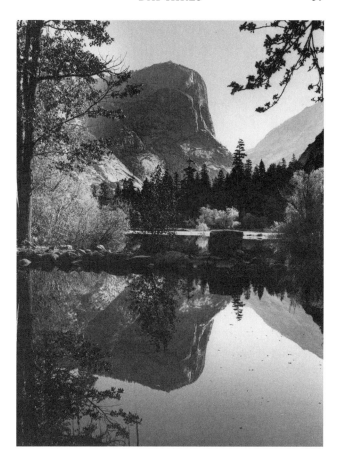

Mirror Lake as it appeared in 1976

From the north side of the bridge a trail climbs briefly north to the Indian Caves area, which you'll visit later. First, however, you take the paved bike path northeast up to a junction with a bike path west to the caves, then you start east and momentarily spy a broad footpath branching left. Chose either route northeast, both reuniting about 0.4 mile later near a shallow pond. Formerly it was deeper and until the mid-1990s was a popular summertime swimming hole. But it is paralleling the evolution of

Glacier polish on cliff near Mirror Lake

adjacent Mirror Lake, reverting to just a broad stretch of
Tenaya Creek. From the north side of the former swimming hole a nature trail loops over to the southwest edge
of former Mirror Lake, as does the main trail, a former
road, which no longer is paved (no bikes here). From the
road's end, a former parking area, is a horse trail that you
can take southwest to Indian Caves or northeast up lower
Tenaya Canyon (see **Day Hike 6**).

In the past, Mirror Lake served a purpose. Tenaya Creek usually dries up by late September, and the Park Service then would excavate up to thousands of tons of sand and gravel from the lake bed to be spread on snow-covered winter roads to make them more driveable. It was an efficient system, but declared environmentally incorrect and stopped in 1971. The lake, after all, was a short-lived rockfall-dammed lake made mirrorlike only with the addition of a dam and then kept deep enough for reflection with the annual removal of sediments.

Today visitors must console themselves with a broad stretch of creek that usually does not mirror Tenaya Canyon, and upon drying, it exposes an unappealing, gravely floor. A grassy meadow may be a long time in coming, and if the creek cuts through the gravelly floor, it will lower the water table, which would allow trees to invade the area and obscure all views.

To resume the loop hike, look for a trail that starts near the back end of the former parking area. (Since it is a heavily used, often smelly, horse trail, you might want to take the previously mentioned foot trail.) Starting south on the horse trail, you see, high above, North Dome and Half Dome. Next the trail passes myriad oversize bounders that fell from the vertical east wall of Washington Column. Soon the trail switchbacks briefly down to the paved bike path, then goes 100 yards west to a trail departing south toward nearby Tenaya Bridge. The trail continues west another 100 yards to enter the unsigned Indian Caves area. Here you can find dozens of caves and dozens of house-size boulders. However, apparently there were too many climbing accidents and too much liability for the Park, so in the early '90s the area officially ceased to exist. If you bring children here, use the utmost caution. Before leaving this area, climb on top of a large, low slab that lies along the trail's north side to find Indian mortar holes used to pulverize acorns.

Continuing west you have a choice: either stay on the trail or take the paved bike path, just south of the caves.

The two diverge and on this stretch you pass under the forbidding south face of Washington Column. Where the trail and bike path come together, near the northeast corner of the former, flood-eradicated Group Camp, you can look up a deep, weathered, vertical fracture that separates Washington Column from that giant lithic rainbow, Royal Arches.

After 150 yards of westward traverse the two parallel paths cross a very low "moraine." Actually, it is an old rockfall deposit similar to one immediately west of the Backpackers Walk-In Campground. About a two-minute walk past it you meet a southbound trail that divides the Group Camp on the east from the Backpackers Walk-In Campground on the west. Taking it you can save 0.3 mile, but by going west for a few minutes along the bike path (the trail goes to the Ahwahnee Hotel), you reach Sugarpine Bridge, named for a huge pine growing by its northeast corner. Like a royal arch, this stately giant could fall any day. From the southeast corner of the bridge you take a trail first southeast up the Merced River, then briefly northeast up Tenaya Creek. Where you meet the southbound trail you take it, immediately bridge Tenaya Creek, and walk southeast beside North Pines Campground to the Valley stables.

DAY HIKE 6
Valley Stables to Lower Tenaya Canyon

Distance: 4.6 to 5.3 miles

Grade: 2A, easy half-day hike

Trailhead: Same as for Day Hike 5. **D1.**

In addition to visiting Mirror Lake, you get varying views of Half Dome and other features in deep, glacier-occupied Tenaya Canyon.

First, follow **Day Hike 5** to the vicinity of former Mirror Lake. If you hike to and return from the lake via the paved bike path—the most popular route—you will hike

4.6 miles. But if you follow all of **Day Hike 5**, you will hike 5.3 miles.

From where a broad trail curves left to a former parking area, you can descend a few steps to the lake's famous viewpoint. In former days, when the lake was deeper, early-morning visitors were treated to a reflection of Mt. Watkins in its still waters. (See **Day Hike 5** for more on this dwindling lake.) Just north of these steps the lower Tenaya Canyon trail begins, and it quickly comes to the northwest arm of the whisp of a lake. About 100 yards beyond it, where the trail bends right, you will come to a 1990s rockfall at the base of a cliff, which has conspicuous polish on it, imparted by a glacier before it retreated up-canyon about 16,000 years ago (see photo on p. 38).

Up-canyon, the fairly level, forested trail soon approaches Tenaya Creek—a good picnic spot. Beyond it you go northeast toward the south spur of Mt. Watkins, which is occasionally seen. About 1.1 miles into the loop you come to a junction with a trail that switchbacks over 100 times in its 2,600-foot climb out of Tenaya Canyon and into its hanging tributary of Snow Creek, described in the author's *Yosemite National Park* guide. Many believe that such canyons became hanging because trunk glaciers eroded their canyons far deeper than tributary glaciers did theirs. However, a hike up treacherous Tenaya Canyon would show that in its steepest parts, where glaciers flowed fastest and should have eroded most, the canyon retains its preglacial **V**-shaped cross section. So in your vicinity, where the floor is flat and glaciers flowed slower, erosion would have been less, and hence the **U**-shaped cross section is preglacial. And indeed, unglaciated, **U**-shaped Sierran canyons—trunk and hanging tributary—do exist.

At most you'll want to ascend only the first dozen switchbacks (which will add to the total mileage) an effort sufficient to get you above the canyon live oaks and present you with a view of Half Dome and much of Tenaya Canyon. From this vantage point in early summer, when the creek flows briskly, you should see Tenaya Creek falls, at about your elevation and about 0.5 mile up-canyon. Return the way you came.

Alternately, from the junction a loop trail used to go 0.3 mile to a bridge over Tenaya Creek. However, the January 1997 flood damaged the bridge and parts of the trail below it, and the trail now is abandoned. If you want to continue ahead, treat it as cross-country. Unless you find a fallen log across Tenaya Creek, you may have to ford it through most of the summer. From the bridge site a use trail heads about 0.3 mile up along the south bank to the creek's falls, whose brim is a worthy goal for safety-minded hikers.

DAY HIKE 7
Big Oak Flat Road Trail
to Cascade Creek

Distance: 7.8 miles round trip

Grade: 2C, strenuous half-day hike

Trailhead: From Crane Flat go east 5.75 miles toward Yosemite Valley down the new Big Oak Flat Road to a trailhead parking area, on your right. If you reach the Foresta road junction, you have gone 0.25 mile too far. The trail begins opposite from the trailhead parking area.

During the late spring, when most of the Park's trails are under snow, this trail is at its best. Views are few and lakes are nonexistent, so it will appeal only to those who want an invigorating yet not exhausting walk and to those who especially focus on nature.

The trail starts a climb northeast (*trail start on map is dated*), and in spring harlequin lupines can abound here, identified by their pink-and-yellow flowers. Later on the flowers will be replaced by pea pods, and nearby Mariposa manzanitas, with their gray-green leaves, will have produced berries. The first third of the route was burned in a 1990 lightning-caused fire, which left charred snags, but it also allowed much more light to reach the ground —hence the profusion of shrubs and wildflowers. Particularly on an initial 400-foot, 0.5-mile climb to a ridge— which has views of El Capitan and Half Dome—dense herbs and shrubs can crowd the trail, and since this vegetation abounds in rodents, it is a prime habitat for rattlesnakes, so watch your step.

In the next 0.5 mile the trail briefly climbs the ridge, then traverses north to a moist area with a seasonal spring. Over the next 0.5 mile you enter unburned forest and then descend to usually flowing Wildcat Creek. Soon you begin to climb again, and do so for almost a mile until you start a short, steep descent along a ridge, which offers a view, across the Merced River canyon, of the Wawona Road traversing the flanks of Turtleback Dome. The steep descent continues down to nearby Tamarack Creek, which in summer flourishes with giant-leaved umbrella plants growing from its stream bed. At times this creek is a wet ford.

Again you make a mile-long climb, then make a momentary drop to a Cascade Creek tributary, which you boulder-hop only yards before reaching the old Big Oak Flat Road. At this creek crossing, service-berries hug the bank of a small pool fed by a photogenic cascade. Once on the road you have a brief walk down to the Cascade Creek bridge—a good spot for a lunch break (camping prohibited). In late summer the flow of Cascade Creek is slow and warm enough for safe and enjoyable splashing around in the small pools immediately downstream. During the summer, when the road to Tamarack Flat Campground is open, you'll want to take the much shorter **Day Hike 8** down to Cascade Creek.

DAY HIKE 8
Tamarack Flat Campground
to Cascade Creek

Distance: 4.4 miles round trip

Grade: 1B, easy half-day hike

Trailhead: From Crane Flat go northeast 3.75 miles up the Tioga Road to the Tamarack Flat Campground turnoff, immediately before the Gin Flat turnout. Go southeast 3.25 miles down the old Big Oak Flat Road to Tamarack Flat Campground's east end. **Above A1.**

Around mid-morning Tamarack Flat Campground can become temporarily abandoned, only to receive another flood of motorized campers in the afternoon. Take the time to enjoy the campground during that tranquil part of day, and while you're in the vicinity, you might take the time to make this pleasant, easy hike.

Some early visitors traveled by stagecoach to Yosemite Valley along this old road, completed it 1874. The first auto entered the Valley in 1900, and the route eventually became well-traveled until the completion of the new Big Oak Flat Road in 1940. Today, the road below the campground is closed to motor vehicles.

Tamarack Flat derives its name from its preponderance of "tamaracks," that is, lodgepole pines. However, as you leave the flat and hike across slopes on the old Big Oak Flat Road, white firs become dominant. Along both sides of the road are large, partly buried granitic boulders. These were not carried here by glaciers; instead, they developed in place, being resistant enough to subsurface weathering that they finally emerged on the surface quite intact, while the adjacent, less resistant, more fractured bedrock was chemically weathered and eroded away.

Just before you reach a prominent cluster of rocks the road begins a steady descent to Cascade Creek. At a switchback just 240 yards before the bridge across this creek, there is a junction with a trail, **Day Hike 7**, that comes from the new Big Oak Flat Road. Along the first 200 yards below its bridge, Cascade Creek splashes down low cascades into small pools, and in late summer these make nice "swimming holes." Before then the creek can be too swift for safe frolicking. Rooted in this creek are large-leaved umbrella plants, and growing just beside the water's edge are creek dogwoods, willows, western azaleas and service-berries.

DAY HIKE 9
El Capitan

Distance: 15.4 miles round trip

Grade: 4D, strenuous day hike

Trailhead: Same as for Day Hike 8. **Above A1.**

The vertical walls of 3,000-foot-high El Capitan attract rock climbers from all over the world, and more than five dozen extremely difficult routes ascend it. For non-climbers this hike provides a much easier, safer way to attain El Capitan's summit, which stands only 15 feet above the north-side approach.

View from summit of El Capitan; Half Dome on left

**El Capitan, the hard way: three climbers (arrows)
about 1,000 feet up the monolith's prow**

Descend to Cascade Creek, as directed in **Day Hike 8**, then continue 0.5 mile down the old Big Oak Flat Road—now more like a trail—to a junction with Yosemite Valley's north rim trail. Or, continue *only* 200 yards below

Cascade Creek to a well-graded, abandoned road, on the left, and follow it 0.25 mile up to the El Capitan trail. Since the Big Oak Flat Road down to the valley floor is quite abandoned, the Park Service ought to also abandon the current trail junction and place it at the junction with the abandoned road. This change will save hikers almost 0.5 mile. From either junction a major climb of almost 2,000 feet confronts you. Along the lands between here and El Capitan, USGS geologist François Matthes mapped seven glacial moraines, extensive, scattered glacial deposits, and 20 glacial erratics. None of the moraines or deposits exist, and all of the erratics are merely locally derived boulders. None of the route ahead was ever glaciated.

Starting in a summer-warm forest, you climb hundreds of feet—steeply at times—up to drier slopes. You then encounter red firs, which grow near the top of a crest. Three miles from the old road, lodgepoles appear as you make a brief descent to a meadow, which you parallel to a crossing of a Ribbon Creek tributary—a wide bog in early summer. This you parallel east a mile down to Ribbon Creek. Ribbon Meadow, which you traverse on the first part of this descent, is more forest than meadow, and blazes on lodgepoles guide you. Along the banks of Ribbon Creek are the trail's only acceptable campsites—but waterless when the creek dries up about midsummer. Now only 1.25 miles from your goal, you make a brief climb, an equally brief descent, and then an ascending traverse east to the top of El Capitan Gully.

Your first views of El Capitan and the south wall of Yosemite Valley appear on the traverse to the gully, and they continue as you climb south from it past dense shrubbery to a junction with the El Capitan spur trail. If you are hiking this trail after Ribbon Creek has dried up, you may want to continue on the main trail 0.5 mile northeast to two trickling springs. The trail beyond them is not all that interesting, but it does get you to Eagle Peak (the long way) and to Yosemite Creek (see **Day Hike 11**).

Along the spur trail south to El Capitan's broad, rounded summit, you can look up-canyon and identify unmistakable Half Dome, at the Valley's end, barely protruding Sentinel Dome, above the Valley's south wall, and fin-shaped Mt. Clark, on the skyline above the dome. Take your time exploring El Capitan's summit area, but don't stray too far. Even some top-notch climbers, after ascending a vertical route, have fallen to their deaths after unroping.

DAY HIKE 10
Yosemite Falls

Distance: 6.6 miles round trip

Grade: 2D, strenuous half-day hike

Trailhead: Park in the westernmost part of the Yosemite Lodge parking lot close to the Camp 4 Walk-In Campground, which is on the north side of the main road. **C1-D1.**

Most Park visitors walk to the base of Lower Yosemite Fall. This popular trail (a knee-knocking descent in reverse) takes you to the other end—the brink of Upper Yosemite Fall. Like other early trails of Yosemite Valley, the Yosemite Falls trail was privately built and then was operated as a toll trail.

From the northwest corner of the parking lot for Camp 4 (Sunnyside) Walk-In Campground, take a trail 120 yards northwest up to the north-side Valley floor trail (**Day Hike 2**). By walking west on it about 25 yards, you reach the start of the Yosemite Falls trail. You leave conifers behind as you start up nearly four dozen switchbacks. Characteristic of old trails, each switchback leg is short. Under the shade of canyon live oaks, which dominate talus slopes like the one you're on, the so-far viewless ascent finally reaches a usually dry wash that provides you with framed views of Leidig Meadow and the Valley's central features.

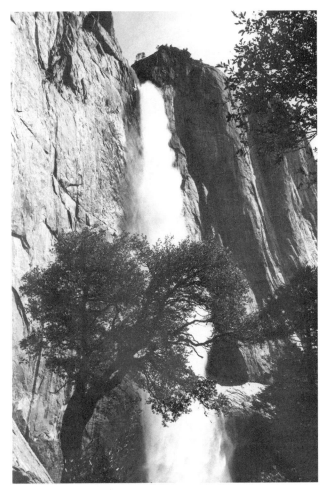

Upper Yosemite Fall, from about switchback 89

With more than one fourth of the elevation gain below you, you pass by more oaks and an occasional bay tree as you now switchback east to a panoramic viewpoint, Columbia Rock, which is a worthy goal in itself. At its safety railing you can study the Valley's geometry, from Half Dome and the Quarter Domes west to the Cathedral Spires. After a few gravely switchbacks climb from the

Lost Arrow Spire, first climbed in 1946

viewpoint, the trail traverses northeast, drops slightly,
then bends north for a sudden, dramatic view of Upper
Yosemite Fall. West of the fall's lower section is a light scar
100 feet high, from which a 1,000-ton rock slab fell, after
being struck by lightning in June 1976. In clear weather in
November 1980, a 4,000-ton slab, probably weakened by

the May 1980 Mammoth Lakes earthquakes, fell from a conspicuous scar on the cliffs west of and above the trail, killing three hikers. Smaller rockfalls have occurred, and over tens of millions of years countless rockfalls—more than glaciers—widened the Valley.

The climb up the long, steep trough ends among white firs and Jeffrey pines, about 135 switchbacks above the Valley floor. Here, in a gully beside a seasonal creeklet, the trail turns right while the Eagle Peak trail, **Day Hike 11**, continues ahead. Your trail makes a brief climb east out of the gully and reaches a broad crest with several overused campsites. Their heavy use puts a strain on this area's vegetation, and it is best not to camp here. Along the crest you follow a trail south almost to the Valley's rim. Then at a juniper you veer east, descend steps almost to Yosemite Creek, and finally descend more steps to a fenced-in viewpoint. If you are acrophobic you should not attempt the last part of this descent, for it is possible, though unlikely, that you could slip on loose gravel and tumble over the brink. Beside the lip of Upper Yosemite Fall you see and hear it plunge all the way down its 1,430-foot drop to the rocks below. Just beyond the fall is a large roof, and beyond it stands the pride of the Clark Range, finlike Mt. Clark.

After returning to the crest campsites you can descend east to a bridge over Yosemite Creek and obtain water. However, be careful! Almost every year one or more persons, wading in it, slip on the glass-smooth creek bottom and are swiftly carried over the fall's brink. From the creek's bridge you could continue eastward 0.75 mile up a trail to Yosemite Point. From that viewpoint a dramatic panorama extends from Clouds Rest south past Half Dome and Glacier Point, then west to the Cathedral Rocks. Near you a massive shaft of rock, Lost Arrow, rises almost to the Valley's rim, and beyond it you can see most of the switchbacking Yosemite Falls trail. See the author's *Yosemite National Park* guide for trail description north from this viewpoint.

DAY HIKE 11
Eagle Peak

Distance: 12.4 miles round trip

Grade: 3E, strenuous day hike

Trailhead: Same as for Day Hike 10. **C1-D1.**

Strategically located Eagle Peak, highest of the Three Brothers, provides commanding views both up and down Yosemite Valley. The hike to it also provides exciting views, including some close-range ones of Upper Yosemite Fall.

Follow **Day Hike 10** up to the Upper Yosemite Fall fenced-in viewpoint, then return to the trail junction in the gully west of the fall. From it you begin a shady trek north, climbing out of the gully, descending into a second, and climbing out of a third to a trail junction. Leaving the Yosemite Creek environs, you climb more than 300 feet, steeply at first, before leveling off in a bouldery area—part of a moraine. This moraine was deposited by a glacier that descended southwest from the west slopes of Mt. Hoffmann. Now you turn south, generally leaving Jeffrey pines and white firs for lodgepole pines and red firs as you climb to Eagle Peak Meadows, whose north edge is blocked by an older moraine.

Beyond the sometimes boggy meadow you cross the headwaters of Eagle Peak Creek and in a few minutes reach a hillside junction. From it an old trail climbs and drops along a 1.75-mile course to the El Capitan spur trail. To reach the summit of that monolith, take the easier route starting from Tamarack Flat Campground (**Day Hike 9**). Branch left from the junction for a moderate 0.6-mile ascent to Eagle Peak's diminutive summit. From the weather-pitted, brushy summit 3,200 feet above the Valley floor, you get far-ranging views that extend all the way to the Sierra crest along the Park's east boundary. Below you, central Yosemite Valley spreads out like a map, and with this book's map you can identify many features.

DAY HIKE 12
Wawona Tunnel to Dewey Point

Distance: 10.9 miles round trip

Grade: 3D, moderate day hike

Trailhead: Discovery View, at the east end of Wawona Tunnel, on the Wawona Road 1.5 miles west of the Bridalveil Fall parking lot entrance. **B1.**

The trail takes you to five viewpoints: Inspiration, Old Inspiration, Stanford, Crocker, and Dewey. The first two, however, are somewhat blocked by vegetation. By hiking only to Stanford Point, you cut about 2.5 miles and 900 feet of climbing from your hike. The creeks found along this route typically dry up by early summer, so make sure you bring sufficient water.

The signed trail starts at the west end of the south-side parking lot and makes a switchbacking, mostly viewless, 500-foot ascent for 0.6 mile to an intersection of the old Wawona Road. Built in 1875, this old stage route got a lot of use before it was closed with the opening of the newer Wawona Road in 1933. Today it provides a quiet descent 1.6 miles down to the newer road, meeting it just 0.3 mile above the entrance to the Bridalveil Fall parking lot.

Beyond the intersection, oaks and conifers shade you up another 500-foot ascent, but also hide most of the scenery. At Inspiration Point you meet a bend in the old Wawona Road, a point where early stage travelers got their first commanding view of El Capitan, Bridalveil Fall, and the Cathedral Rocks. Today incense-cedars, oaks, and pines obstruct the view. Pushing onward, you gain 1,200 feet on the Pohono Trail, encountering sugar pines, white firs, and sporadic Douglas-firs before arriving at Artist Creek.

Now at an elevation with pleasant afternoon temperatures, you make a steep 300-foot climb to Old Inspiration Point, whose view is partly blocked. The actual point, identified on the map, is on the projecting spur below and northwest of you, and before construction of the old Wawona Road, a stock trail offered access to it.

Red firs now add shade to the forest canopy as you briefly ascend before dropping to a welcome spring and nearby Meadow Brook. If any water remains along this trail through midsummer, it will be found here. Beyond the creek and its alders you head north and soon descend to the first significant viewpoint, at the end of a short spur trail—Stanford Point. From it you see the gaping chasm of western Yosemite Valley and can easily identify its prominent landmarks: Leaning Tower, Bridalveil Fall, the Cathedral Rocks, El Capitan and, seasonally, Ribbon Fall. If you are not yet exhausted, the power of this view will urge you to climb 0.5 mile farther, reaching Crocker Point after more than 400 feet of elevation gain. This point, on the brink of an overhanging cliff, provides a heart-pounding view similar to the last one, though better. Now most of the Valley's famed landmarks stand boldly before you, and you look over and beyond all the Cathedral Rocks to see the Three Brothers. To the left of Clouds Rest lie twin-towered Cathedral Peak and broad-topped Mt. Hoffmann, with distant Mt. Conness between them, marking the Sierra crest along the Park's northeast boundary.

For rival views, continue 0.6 mile to the hike's end at slightly higher 7385-foot Dewey Point. Just east of this point, François Matthes of the U.S. Geological Survey mapped ancient glacial deposits up to 7000 feet elevation, indicating glaciers deep enough to bury the Cathedral Rocks. Unfortunately, none of his evidence actually exists, and neither did his glaciers. Now closer to the Cathedral Rocks, the perspective is different, and you look straight down the massive face that supports Leaning Tower. Also intriguing is the back side of Middle Cathedral Rock, with an iron-rich, rust-stained surface. Finally, you see the Cathedral Spires head-on so they appear as one.

DAY HIKE 13
Bridalveil Campground to Dewey Point

Distance: 10.0 miles round trip

Grade: 3C, moderate half-day hike

Trailhead: Branch from the Wawona Road and drive 7.6 miles up the Glacier Point Road to the Bridalveil Creek Campground road. Turn right and drive 0.5 mile to the campground's entrance. **C2.**

This is the easier of two routes to scenic Dewey Point, and it requires less than half the climbing effort of the previous hike. But then, it doesn't visit Stanford and Crocker points.

At the entrance to Bridalveil Campground a closed road departs southwest away from the camp's Loop A. On it you soon cross a creek that drains Westfall Meadows, then immediately meet a trail. Heading south, this undesirable trail passes through these meadows, then makes a brush-choked descent to an old logging area—a 1920s "battleground" between environmentalists and the Yosemite Lumber Company. The environmentalists won, but the impact from logging lingers on.

Rather than head south you take a trail north, which climbs gently over old, weathered terrain to the Glacier Point Road. By starting here—0.25 mile west of the campground's road—you would cut 1.75 miles off the round-trip distance. From the road the lodgepole-shaded trail gently descends almost to the north tip of largely hidden Peregoy Meadow before topping a low divide, and then it drops moderately to the south edge of McGurk Meadow. In this sedge-rich, sometimes flowery meadow (usually just after the snow has melted), the route bridges its creek.

From the meadow you see the low summits of the Ostrander Rocks to the east, and then at the meadow's north end re-enter dense lodgepole forest. The trail soon crests at a shallow, viewless saddle, then descends moderately to gently to a low-crest trail fork. The fork right quickly joins the Pohono Trail and drops to Bridalveil Creek, with water year-round. You fork left, quickly join the Pohono Trail, start west on it and, near a broad, low divide (camping hereabouts), traverse a dry, gravely slope.

The forest cover now becomes dominated by firs, and on the damp shady floor beneath them you may find white-veined wintergreen, snow plant and spotted coralroot, all deriving nutrients to varying degrees from soil fungi. Two Bridalveil Creek tributaries are crossed, then a smaller third one before you start up a fourth that drains a curving gully. On its upper slopes Jeffrey pine, huckleberry oak, and greenleaf manzanita replace firs, and in a few minutes you reach prized Dewey Point, described at the end of **Day Hike 12**. If you can get someone to meet you at the Wawona Tunnel, then descend to it along this highly scenic portion of the Pohono Trail.

DAY HIKE 14
The Fissures at Taft Point

Distance: 2.6 miles round trip

Grade: 1A, easy 2-hour hike

Trailhead: Branch from the Wawona Road and drive 13.2 miles up the Glacier Point Road to a scenic turnout, on your left, which is 2.3 miles before the Glacier Point parking-lot entrance. **D1.**

The views from Taft Point rival those from Glacier Point. However, since Taft Point is reached by trail, it is much less visited than is Glacier Point. Generally lacking protective railings, Taft Point and the Fissures are potentially dangerous, so don't bring along children unless you can really keep them under strict control.

From the road-cut parking area you descend about 50 yards to a trail, turn left, and start southwest on it. After about 150 yards of easy descent you pass a trailside outcrop that is almost entirely composed of glistening

Fissures at overhanging Taft Point

whitish-gray quartz. It also has small amounts of pink potassium feldspar. In a minute you come to seasonal Sentinel Creek, whose limited drainage area keeps Sentinel Fall downstream from being one of Yosemite Valley's prime attractions. After boulder-hopping the creek you follow an undulating trail west past pines, firs, and brush to a broad-saddle junction with the Pohono Trail (**Day Hike 16**). Just north of it you'll notice some large, weathered boulders. Not left by glaciers, these boulders weathered in place and will stand higher and higher above their surroundings as the surrounding bedrock is weathered away at a faster rate.

From the junction you descend to a sometimes seeping creeklet that drains through a small field of corn lilies. Descending toward the Fissures, you cross drier slopes that are generally covered with brush. Soon you arrive at the Fissures—five vertical, parallel fractures that cut through overhanging Profile Cliff, beneath your feet. Beyond them you walk up to a small railing at the brink of an obvious point and get an acrophobia-inducing view of overhanging Profile Cliff, beneath you. For the best views of Yosemite Valley and the High Sierra walk west to exposed Taft Point, from where you see the Cathedral spires and rocks, El Capitan, the Three Brothers, Yosemite Falls, and Sentinel Rock. Broad-topped Mt. Hoffmann stands on the skyline just east of Indian Canyon, and east of that peak stands distant Mt. Conness, on the Sierra crest.

DAY HIKE 15
Sentinel Dome

Distance: 2.4 miles round trip

Grade: 1B, moderate 2-hour hike

Trailhead: Same as for Day Hike 14. **D1.**

Sentinel Dome rivals Half Dome as the most-climbed dome in the Park. Tuolumne Meadows' Lembert and Pothole domes rival them, but neither is a true dome; each is a *roche moutonnée*—an asymmetrical, glacier-smoothed ridge. Indeed, most of the Sierra's domes, glaciated *or* unglaciated, are asymmetrical ridges.

From the road-cut parking area you descend about 50 yards to a trail, turn right and make a curving, generally ascending traverse 0.75 mile north almost to the south base of Sentinel Dome. Here you meet and briefly hike north on a road, which has several large boulders along it. These, and ones between this dome and Glacier Point, supposedly were left by ancient glaciers. They were not;

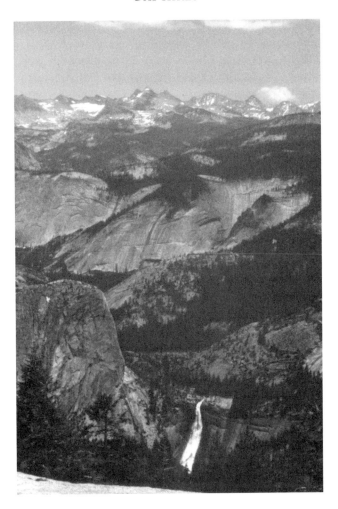

View east from Sentinel Dome

the boulders are locally derived. No glacier ever filled Yosemite Valley to its rim. On the road you soon come to a fork, where you veer left, and in 30 yards, at another fork, veer left again. In a few minutes you arrive at the dome's north end, where you meet a path from Glacier Point. You now climb southwest up quite safe, unexposed bedrock slopes to the summit.

At an elevation of 8,122 feet, Sentinel Dome is the second highest viewpoint above Yosemite Valley. Only Half Dome—a strenuous hike—is higher. Seen from the summit, El Capitan, Yosemite Falls, and Half Dome stand out as the three most prominent Valley landmarks. West of Half Dome are two bald features, North and Basket domes. On the skyline above North Dome stands blocky Mt. Hoffmann, the Park's geographic center, while to the east, above Mt. Starr King (an unglaciated, true dome) stands the rugged crest of the Clark Range. In years past almost everyone who climbed Sentinel Dome expected to photograph its windswept, solitary Jeffrey pine, made famous by Ansel Adams. That tree, unfortunately, finally succumbed to vandalism in 1984.

DAY HIKE 16
South Rim Traverse

Distance: 13.5 miles one way

Grade: 3D, moderate day hike

Trailhead: Branch from the Wawona Road and drive 15.5 miles up the Glacier Point Road to its end. If possible, take a Park bus up to crowded Glacier Point. **D1.**

This hike, the Pohono Trail, takes you past several excellent viewpoints, each showing a different part of Yosemite Valley in a unique perspective. After early June carry enough water (usually one quart) to last you until midpoint, Bridalveil Creek, which is the hike's only permanent source of water.

On the low crest just east of the entrance to the Glacier Point parking lot, you start south up a signed trail that quickly forks. **Day Hike 18** branches left but you branch right and under white-fir cover momentarily cross the Glacier Point Road. Beyond it you immediately branch right again since the path ahead climbs to a ranger's residence. The still-climbing trail curves west up to a switchback, then south to a road. This you cross and continue up the relentless grade to a north-descending crest which you cross before climbing briefly south to a gully. In it, almost a mile from Glacier Point, you are faced with a choice. The route, the Pohono Trail, goes west to the brink of Sentinel Fall—usually dry by midsummer—while the alternate route, which starts north before climbing south, goes to scenic Sentinel Dome. Should you take the dome route, you can return to the Pohono Trail or you can take a more level route that adds 0.6 mile to the total distance. From the dome this route follows **Day Hike 15** in reverse, then the first half of **Day Hike 14**, which takes you back to the Pohono Trail.

The main route, the Pohono Trail, leaves the gully, traverses southwest across a lower face of Sentinel Dome, then drops to a gravely gully with north-side boulders. The gravel and boulders here, like all between Glacier Point and Sentinel Dome, are locally derived, not lingering deposits left by an ancient glacier. The route stays gravelly on a short, sometimes steep descent to Sentinel Creek. There you can follow its bank 90 yards out to a point to get a good Valley view. Before mid-June hikers will see upper Sentinel Fall splashing down a chute immediately west of the point.

Beyond the seasonal creek you climb past lodgepole pines and white firs, and then, before a broad-saddle junction, past Jeffrey pines and red firs. At the junction you rejoin the alternate route and, as in the second half of **Day Hike 14**, descend a trail to the Fissures and Taft Point. Be careful when exploring this scenic though precipitous area. From the westernmost fissure the Pohono Trail descends south, then contours west to a low ridge. By following the ridge about 250 yards out to its end you'll reach an unnamed point that gives you a view down upon the Cathedral Rocks, lined up in a row. Descending from the low ridge, the shady Pohono Trail drops 700 feet to a bridge over Bridalveil Creek. Level ground is limited, so if you plan to camp, you can get water here, and perhaps camp in isolated spots on lands north and west of two nearby trail junctions.

From the creek, which is the hike's approximate mid-point, you climb shortly west to these two junctions with a lateral trail. This one climbs 2 miles south to the Glacier Point Road, then a short mile beyond it to Bridalveil Campground. This lateral trail constitutes the first half of **Day Hike 13** (described in the northward direction), and turning to the second half of that hike's description, you let it guide you over to Dewey Point. West from that point you follow **Day Hike 12**, described in the reverse direction, down to Discovery View, at the east end of Wawona Tunnel.

DAY HIKE 17

Glacier Point to Yosemite Valley via Four Mile Trail

Distance: 4.6 miles one way

Grade: IA, easy 2-hour hike

Trailhead: Same as for Day Hike I6. **D1.**

This trail provides a very scenic descent to Yosemite Valley—a descent that will acquaint you with the Valley's main features. This knee-knocking descent also gives you a feel for the Valley's 3000-foot depth.

Before building the Yosemite Falls trail (**Day Hike 10**) John Conway first worked on this trail, completing it in 1872. Originally about four miles long, it was rebuilt and lengthened in 1929 but the trail's name stuck. The trail starts west from the north side of a concessionaire's shop, entering a shady bowl whose white firs and sugar pines usually harbor snow patches well into June. You then con-tour northwest, eventually emerge from forest shade and, looking east, see unglaciated Glacier Point's two over-hanging rocks capping a vertical wall. Soon you curve west, veer in and out of a cool gully, then reach a descend-ing ridge. Switchbacks begin, and where gravel lies on hard tread, one can easily take a minor spill if not careful.

Brush dominates the first dozen switchback legs, thereby giving you unobstructed panoramas, though making the hike a hot one for anyone ascending from the Valley floor on a summer afternoon. However, as you duck east into a gully, shady conifers appear, though they somewhat censor the views. About midway down the series of switchbacks, canyon live oaks begin to compete with white firs and Douglas-firs, and the view is obstructed even more. After descending two thirds of the vertical distance to the Valley floor, the switchbacks temporarily end. A long, steady descent now ensues, mostly past canyon live oaks, whose curved-upward trunks are their response to creeping talus. (The talus has been erroneously mapped by the U.S. Geological Survey as glacial deposits.) Black oaks and incense-cedars also appear, and after 0.25 mile you cross a creeklet that usually flows until early July. Down it you have an excellent view of Leidig Meadow. The steady descent again enters oak cover and you skirt below the base of imposing but largely hidden Sentinel Rock. At last a final group of switchbacks guide you down to a former parking loop, closed about 1975, and you proceed north, intersecting the Valley floor's southside trail, **Day Hike 2**, halfway to the end point, Southside Drive.

Walk the Sequoia woods at any time of the year and you will say they are the most beautiful and majestic on earth. Beautiful and impressive contrasts meet you everywhere—the colors of tree and flower, rock and sky, light and shade, strength and frailty, endurance and evanescence. . . .
— John Muir

DAY HIKE 18
Glacier Point to Yosemite Valley via Nevada and Vernal Falls

Distance: 9.1 miles one way

Grade: 2C, moderate day hike

Trailhead: Same as for Day Hike 16. **D1.**

This is the most scenic of all trails descending to the floor of Yosemite Valley. Either take a bus up to Glacier Point or have someone drop you there and meet you down at Camp Curry.

Just east of the entrance to the Glacier Point parking lot, you start south up a signed trail that quickly forks. The Pohono Trail, **Day Hike 16**, veers right, but you veer left, climbing a bit more before starting a moderate descent. A switchback leg helps ease the grade, and then you descend, often with views. A 1987 natural fire blackened most of the forest from near the trailhead to just beyond the upcoming Buena Vista Trail junction, but most trees survived. In open areas, black oaks are thriving, and shrubs have regenerated with a vengeance. Between charred trunks are occasional great views of Half Dome, Mt. Broderick, Liberty Cap, Nevada Fall, and Mt. Starr King. After 1.6 miles and an 800-foot drop, the Glacier Point-Panorama Trail meets the Buena Vista Trail. Over 2.2 miles this first heads up-canyon to Illilouette Creek, then leads up along it to intersect the Mono Meadow Trail (**Backpack Hike 4**).

Your trail branches left and switchbacks down to a spur trail that goes a few yards to a railing. Here, atop an overhanging cliff, you get an unobstructed view of 370-foot-high Illilouette Fall, which splashes down over a low point on the rim of massive Panorama Cliff. Behind it Half Dome rises boldly while above Illilouette Creek Mt. Starr King rises even higher. In 0.25 mile the trail descends to a wide bridge, wisely placed upstream. Still,

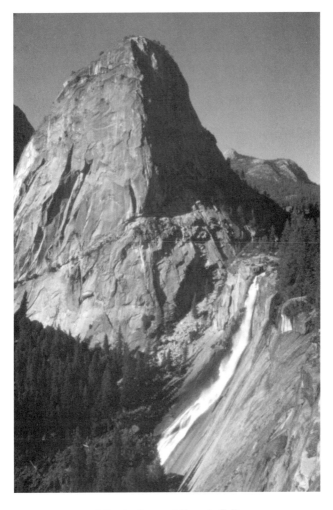

Liberty Cap and Nevada Fall

wading in the creek could carry you swiftly downstream and over the fall.

The trail soon passes just above the brink of Illilouette Fall, and gravels here are remnants of a thick accumulation that choked the creek when the uppermost part of the last glacier formed a low ice-dam across its mouth.

The trail then starts a major climb along the slopes just above Panorama Cliff. It first climbs briefly along its rim, then switchbacks away, soon returning near Panorama Point. The former viewpoint was in part undermined by a monstrous rockfall that broke loose during the winter of 1968–69. The rest of the viewpoint could break loose at any time. About 0.3 mile past this vicinity you have a superlative panorama extending from Upper Yosemite Fall east past Royal Arches, Washington Column, and North Dome to Half Dome. The forested, moderate climb ends after 200 more feet of elevation gain, and then you descend gently to the rim for some more views, contour east and have even more, these dominated by Half Dome, Mt. Broderick, Liberty Cap, Clouds Rest, and Nevada Fall. The contour ends at a junction with the Mono Meadow Trail, which climbs southwest over a low ridge before descending to Illilouette Creek.

Beyond the junction you make a mile-long, switchbacking, generally viewless descent to a trail split, each branch descending a few yards to the John Muir Trail. You'll descend along it, as described in the last part of **Day Hike 20**, but first walk over to the nearby brink of roaring Nevada Fall. Alternately, you could descend the Mist Trail, a shorter route, which begins a few hundred yards northeast of Nevada Fall. Being shorter, it is also steeper, and is potentially dangerous for those who try to descend it too rapidly. This wet route is described in the opposite direction in the first part of **Day Hike 20**. From the reunion of the John Muir and the Mist trails, you walk but a minute to the Vernal Fall bridge, then follow **Day Hike 19** in reverse down to the Happy Isles shuttle-bus stop. From it you can ride or walk west to Camp Curry, the Valley's east hub of activity.

DAY HIKE 19
Vernal Fall Bridge

Distance: 1.6 miles round trip

Grade: 1A, moderate 2-hour hike

Trailhead: Happy Isles shuttle-bus stop in eastern Yosemite Valley. **D1.**

Popular, paved paths go to near the bases of Yosemite and Bridalveil falls, and a paved one goes to this bridge. If you have only one day here, take all three. The trail to the bridge, however, is steep—intimidating for out-of-shape flatlanders.

From the shuttle-bus stop you walk briefly east across an adjacent bridge and head south, soon reaching the start of the famous John Muir Trail, which heads about 210 miles southward to the summit of Mt. Whitney. After a few minutes up it you meet a trail on the right that descends to the nearby Merced River. In a few more yards you reach a small spring with questionably pure water.

Beyond it the climb south steepens, and before bending east you get a glance back at Upper Yosemite Fall, partly blocked by the Glacier Point Apron. This smooth, curving apron contrasts with the generally angular nature of Yosemite's topography. Note the canyon wall south of the apron, which has a series of oblique-angle cliffs—all of them remarkably similar in orientation since they've fractured along the same series of joint planes. At the canyon's end Illilouette Fall plunges 370 feet over a vertical, joint-controlled cliff. Just east of the fall is a large, light-colored scar that marks the site of a major rockfall that broke loose during the winter of 1968–69.

Climbing east you head up a canyon whose floor in times past was buried by as much as 2,000 feet of glacier ice. Hiking beneath the unstable, highly fractured south wall of Sierra Point, you cross a talus slope—an accumulation of rockfall boulders. The May 1980 Mammoth Lakes earthquakes perhaps set up three rockfalls here,

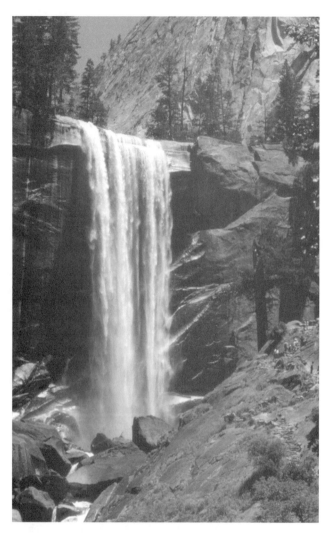

Vernal Fall and hikers on Mist Trail

which finally occurred in conjunction with heavy rains in late spring 1986. More may occur. Entering forest shade once more, you first struggle up the steep trail before making a quick drop to your destination, the Vernal Fall bridge. From it you see Vernal Fall—a broad curtain of water—plunge 320 feet over a vertical cliff before cascading toward you. Looming above the fall are two glacier-resistant masses, Mt. Broderick (left) and Liberty Cap (right). Just beyond the bridges are restrooms and an emergency telephone (heart attacks, slips on dangerous rocks). **Day Hike 20** continues onward.

DAY HIKE 20
Vernal–Nevada Falls Loop

Distance: 5.9 miles semiloop trip

Grade: 2D, strenuous half-day hike

Trailhead: Same as for Day Hike 19. **D1.**

Mile for mile, this very popular hike may be the most scenic one in the Park. The first part of this loop goes up the famous (or infamous) Mist Trail—a steep, strenuous trail that sprays you with Vernal Fall's mist, which cools you on hot afternoons but makes the mostly bedrock route slippery and dangerous. Take rain gear or, if it is a warm day, strip down to swimwear, since you can dry out on slabs above the fall. For best photos start after 10 a.m.

Day Hike 19 tells you what to expect along the hike up to the Vernal Fall bridge. About 200 yards beyond the bridge you come to the start of the loop. Here the Mist Trail continues upriver while the John Muir Trail starts a switchbacking ascent to the right. This is the route taken by those with horses or other pack stock. You'll go up the Mist Trail and down the John Muir Trail. You can, of course go up or down either, but by starting the loop up the Mist Trail, you stand less chance of an accident. Hikers are more apt to slip or to twist an ankle descending than ascending, and the Mist Trail route to Nevada Fall has ample opportunities for mishaps.

In swimsuit or raingear you start up the Mist Trail and soon, rounding a bend, receive your first spray. If you're climbing this trail on a sunny day, you're almost certain to

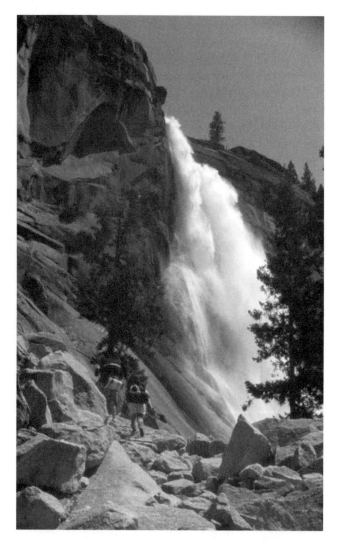

Backpackers heading toward Nevada Fall

see one, if not two, rainbows come alive in the fall's spray. The spray increases as you advance toward the fall, but you get a brief respite behind a large boulder. Beyond it you complete the 300-plus steps, most of them wet, which guide you up through a verdant, spray-drenched garden.

You struggle up the last few dozen steps under the shelter of trees, then, reaching an alcove beneath an ominous overhang, scurry left up a last set of stairs. These, protected by a railing, guide you to the top of a vertical cliff. Pausing here you can study the route, the nearby fall, and the river gorge. The railing ends near the brink of Vernal Fall, but unfortunately, people venture beyond it, and every year it seems that one or more are swept over the fall.

Plunging into the upper end of chilly Emerald Pool is churning Silver Apron. Late in the summer when the Merced's flow is noticeably down, one is tempted to glide down this watery chute into Emerald Pool. This is hazardous, for one can easily crash on some boulders just beyond the end of this silvery chute. Rivers are not to be taken lightly. You'll see a bridge spanning the narrow gorge that confines the Silver Apron, and this structure is your immediate goal. The trail can be vague in this area for so many paths have been trampled through it, but the route leaves the river near the pool's far (east) end, and you'll find outhouses here. After a brief climb south, the trail angles east to a nearby junction. From it a view-packed trail climbs almost 0.5 mile to Clark Point, where it meets the John Muir Trail. You, however, stay low and curve left over to the Silver Apron bridge. Beyond it you have a short, moderate climb up to a broad bench which was once the site of La Casa Nevada. Opened in 1870 it was managed by Albert Snow until 1891, when a fire burned the main structure to the ground.

Spurred onward by the sight and sound of plummeting Nevada Fall, you climb eastward, soon commencing a series of more than two dozen compact switchbacks. As you ascend them, Nevada Fall slips out of view, but you can see towering Liberty Cap. The climb ends at the top of a joint-controlled gully where, on brushy slopes, you once again meet the John Muir Trail (with outhouses just up it—see **Day Hike 21**). From this junction you head southwest toward nearby Nevada Fall. Along this stretch you may notice boulders—rich in large, blocky feldspar crystals—that contrast strongly with the local bedrock. These boulders are erratics—that is, rocks left by retreating glaciers which were here perhaps as recently as 16,000 years ago. Near the Merced River are patches of bedrock that have been polished, striated, and gouged by the last glacier.

Just a few yards before the Nevada Fall bridge you can strike northwest on a short spur trail down to a viewpoint beside the fall's brink. This viewpoint's railing is seen from the fall's bridge, thereby giving you an idea where the trail ends. Don't stray along the cliff's edge and, as said earlier, respect the river—people have been swept over this fall too. Standing near the tumultuous brink of the Merced River, you can look across its canyon—minimally eroded by glaciers—to unglaciated Glacier Point. Vernal Fall, which lies just beyond Emerald Pool, plunges over a vertical wall that is perpendicular to the steep one Nevada Fall plunges over. This part of the canyon contains major fracture planes, or joint planes, which account for the canyon's angular landscape.

From the Nevada Fall bridge you strike southwest, immediately passing more glacier polish and erratic boulders, and shortly ending a gentle ascent at a junction just beyond a seeping spring. Here you meet the Glacier Point-Panorama Trail, and those descending from Glacier Point (**Day Hike 18**) join you here for a descent to Happy Isles along the John Muir Trail. You start with a high traverse that provides an ever-changing panorama of domelike Liberty Cap and broad-topped Mt. Broderick—both testaments to the ineffectiveness of glacial erosion. As you progress west, Half Dome becomes prominent, its hulking mass vying for your attention. Eventually you descend to Clark Point, where you meet a scenic connecting trail that switchbacks down to Emerald Pool.

Backpackers, packers, and those wishing to keep dry continue down the John Muir Trail, which curves south into a gully, switchbacks down to the base of spreading Panorama Cliff, then switchbacks down a talus slope. Largely shaded by canyon live oaks and Douglas-firs, it reaches a junction with a horse trail (no hikers allowed) that descends to the Valley's stables. You continue a brief minute more to a junction with the Mist Trail, turn left and quickly reach the Vernal Fall bridge, from which you retrace your steps.

DAY HIKE 21
Half Dome via Little Yosemite Valley

Distance: 16.4 miles round trip

Grade: 4E, strenuous day hike

Trailhead: Same as for Day Hike 19. **D1.**

Half Dome "is a crest of granite rising to the height of 4,737 feet above the Valley, perfectly inaccessible, being probably the only one of all the prominent points about the Yosemite which never has been and never will be trodden by human foot." So wrote Josiah D. Whitney—California's first prominent geologist—in his 1870 Yosemite Guide-Book. Just five years later the impossible was accomplished, when George Anderson labored for weeks drilling a row of holes up to the "inaccessible" summit, reached on October 12, 1875. In the 1990s, hundreds reach the summit virtually every sunny summer day. The dome is being loved to death, and perhaps the day will come when the cables up it will be dismantled, leaving the summit to the realm of climbers.

Try to start by 7 a.m., following **Day Hike 20** up the Mist Trail or the John Muir Trail to a junction just northeast of the brink of Nevada Fall. If you take the former, you will save 1.0 mile. From the junction and its adjacent outhouses you ascend a brushy, rocky gully, then quickly descend, reaching both forest shade and the Merced River. Beneath pines, firs, and incense-cedars you continue northeast along the river's azalea-lined bank, then quickly reach a trail fork. The left fork saves you 0.1 mile, but you'll expend as much energy as on the right fork due to the climb to vault Liberty Cap's low east ridge. You keep

Hikers descending Half Dome's intimidating cable route

to the main trail and go a short 0.5 mile to another junction, from where the John Muir Trail/Half Dome Trail branches north, while the Merced Lake Trail continues east. On the short stretch north to the left fork, you pass first a large camping area with bearproof storage boxes, then outhouses, and beyond them a spur trail northeast over to a rangers' camp. Some hikers on their way to Half Dome or Merced Lake (**Backpack Hike 1**) spend their first night here.

From the junction with the left fork, you've not yet expended half the energy required to reach the summit. After 1.3 miles of forested ascent you leave the John Muir Trail, which climbs east to Tuolumne Meadows (see the *Hiker's Guide to the High Sierra: Tuolumne Meadows*), and continue up the Half Dome Trail. After 0.6 mile you meet a spur trail that goes about 280 yards east to a spring—your last chance for water (treat it!). The trail bends west before reaching a saddle, and then it climbs through a forest of red firs and Jeffrey pines instead of white firs and incense-cedars. Half Dome's northeast face comes into view and, topping a crest, you get a fine view of Clouds Rest and its satellites, the Quarter Domes. Between them and you, previous glaciers spilled into Tenaya Canyon.

A crest traverse reveals more views, then it ends all too soon at the base of Half Dome's shoulder, where a sign warns you of the potential lightning hazard. Even when thunderstorms are miles away, static electricity can build up on the summit. Out of a clear blue sky a charge can bolt down the cable, throwing your arms off it—or worse. If your hair starts standing on end, beat a hasty retreat!

Almost two dozen short switchbacks guide you up the view-blessed ridge of the dome's shoulder and, near the top, a cable lends additional aid. A real danger on this section is loose gravel, which could prove fatal if you fell off the trail at an exposed spot. Topping the shoulder you are confronted with the famous, intimidating Half Dome cables. (Usually the cables are put up around mid-May and removed in early October.) The ascent starts out gently enough, but it too quickly steepens almost to a 45° angle. On this stretch, first-timers often slow to a snail's pace, clenching both cables with sweaty hands.

The rarefied air certainly hinders your progress as you struggle upward, but an easing gradient gives new incentive and soon you are scrambling up to the broad summit area about the size of 17 football fields. With caution most hikers proceed to the dome's high point (8,842 feet), located at the north end, from where they can view the dome's overhanging northwest point. Stout-hearted souls

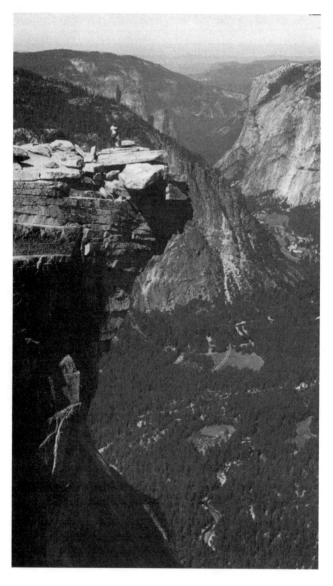

Hiker on Half Dome summit

peer over the lip of this point for an adrenaline-charged view down the dome's 2,000-foot-high northwest face, perhaps seeing climbers ascending it. In the past a few folks liked to camp overnight to view the sunrise, but in 1993 camping became banned in order to protect the small population of Mt. Lyell salamanders.

From the broad summit of this monolith, which originated in the late days of the dinosaurs, you have a 360° panorama. You can look down Yosemite Valley to the bald brow of El Capitan and up Tenaya Canyon past Clouds Rest to Cathedral Peak, the Sierra crest, and Mt. Hoffmann. Mt. Starr King—a dome that rises only 250 feet above you—dominates the Illilouette Creek basin to the south, while the Clark Range cuts the sky to the southeast. Looking due east across Moraine Dome's summit, one sees Mt. Florence, whose broad form hides the Park's highest peak, Mt. Lyell, behind it.

DAY HIKE 22
Alder Creek Trail to Bishop Creek

Distance: 6.3 miles round trip

Grade: 2C, moderate half-day hike

Trailhead: On the Wawona Road 3.9 miles north of the Wawona Campground entrance and 280 yards west of the Alder Creek crossing; also 7.4 miles south of the Glacier Point Road junction. **B4.**

The descent to Bishop Creek can be one of the Sierra's most pleasant springtime hikes, though by early summer the creeks run dry and temperatures soar. Most of this trail's length is across rolling topography carpeted with one of the author's favorite plants, mountain misery; nowhere else in the Park will you see such a spread of this low, aromatic shrub.

From the road's bend near a cut through weathered granite, the trail drops below the Wawona Road and parallels it northwest. The trail quickly widens along an

Manzanita and ponderosa pine along the Alder Creek Trail

abandoned road, which it momentarily leaves. After about 0.5 mile of traversing, it begins a long drop to the South Fork Merced River. About 1.2 miles from the trailhead, you leave the Park and in the Sierra National Forest descend 0.8 mile to a springtime creek. In a short 0.25 mile beyond it you climb to a low ridge, on which you'll find about a half dozen Indian mortar holes, perhaps covered with black-oak leaves, just a few yards west of the trail. From the ridge you have a steady descent, one that winds in and out of gullies as it drops about 550 feet to the banks of Bishop Creek. From there you could continue down to the South Fork Merced River—a total drop of almost 800 feet along a dry, steep 1.4-mile course. However, the steepness, heat, riverside litter, and springtime ticks make the descent not worth it.

DAY HIKE 23
Chilnualna Falls

Distance: 8.1 miles round trip

Grade: 2D, moderate day hike

Trailhead: At the east end of the Chilnualna Road. The Chilnualna Road starts in the Wawona area immediately north of the bridge across the South Fork Merced River. On it you drive past the Pioneer Yosemite History Center, horse stables (trail rides), and a nearby fork right to the Park's district office. In 0.1 mile another road forks left, and just beyond it, on the right, is a small parking area for the Alder Creek Trail, located 0.5 mile along the road. This northbound trail begins roughly 100 yards east of the road forking left. You then drive east 1.25 miles farther, to a short road branching down to a large parking area. This road is located only 100 yards before the pavement on Chilnualna Road ends. Ahead, a dirt road descends to bridge Chilnualna Creek, while a paved road curves northwest. From the parking area a trail climbs about 100 yards north-northeast to the actual trailhead. If you have stock, you will have to head about 250 yards up the paved road curving northwest to a road climbing north. Ascend this 0.25 mile to its second switchback, from where a horse trail climbs about 280 yards east to the end of the foot trail. **C5.**

Not all waterfalls are found in Yosemite Valley; several are located along Chilnualna Creek. As in the Valley, the severely hanging canyon of Chilnualna Creek above the highest fall originated tens of millions of years ago, not in response to glaciers deeply eroding the South Fork Merced River canyon, because they didn't do that.

The hikers' trail starts as a gently ascending dirt road, quickly giving way to a footpath that heads up Chilnualna Creek almost to its 25-foot-high fall. When the creek's flow is slow, hikers with some climbing skill can follow the creek several hundred yards up to a fairly large swimming hole, at the base of another fall. Most stick to the trail, which becomes steep and potentially dangerous, especially when wet. Soon it reaches the horse trail, and on it you climb to cross a manzanita-clothed ridge before entering a forest of ponderosa pines and incense-cedars. A few open spots allow you to survey the Wawona area to the south, Wawona Point to the southeast, and Wawona Dome to the east. Then climbing east you reach Chilnualna Creek in 0.25 mile, and hike up along it another 0.25 mile. If you need water, get it before the trail leaves the creek. In mid and late summer the ascent can be hot and dry.

On a moderately graded trail you now climb more than a dozen switchbacks of various lengths up into a cooler forest before making a fairly open traverse southeast toward the main Chilnualna Fall. Here you see the entire length of the fall, which churns for hundreds of feet down a deep, confining chute. The trail comes to within a few yards of the fall's brink, but due to loose gravel and lack of a protective railing, you should not venture any closer to it.

Not far above Chilnualna Fall proper is an upper fall, a 60-foot-high cascade that is quite impressive in early season. To get around this fall and its small gorge, the trail switchbacks north, then curves south above the lip of the gorge. Views extending over the forested Wawona area are left behind as you reach a trail junction. Just below this junction and also below the main trail east of it are several good campsites. From the junction **Backpack Hike 5** follows the trail climbing generally northeast up Chilnualna Creek, while **Backpack Hike 2** follows the trail that descends south to here from Turner Meadows.

DAY HIKE 24
Wawona to Mariposa Grove

Distance: 16.2+ miles round trip

Grade: 4D, strenuous day hike

Trailhead: In Wawona, take the eastbound road that goes along the south side of the South Fork Merced River. This first passes a parking area on the right, then soon reaches an RV dump station on the left. Continue east 160 yards farther to a road branching right, west-southwest. Make a tight turn onto it and follow it to where it curves south and almost levels off. The trail begins immediately before the road crosses the high point of a west-dropping ridge. **B5.**

Though almost all Mariposa Grove visitors drive to it, one can also walk to it. This hike describes the forested pathway to the Mariposa Grove of Big Trees (giant sequoias)—or Wawona, as the Indians called them.

The trail, initially part of the Two Hour Ride Trail, begins eastward as a dusty horse trail locally adorned with excrement, urine, and flies. You quickly pass an old, abandoned canal, climb to the crest, and in a short mile reach a crest fork. To the left, a broad horse path descends to a summer camp. From it the broad horse path climbs southeast back up to a junction with the trail. This junction is reached after a second short, dusty mile, most of it right along the forested crest. Views of large Wawona meadow are generally poor or nonexistent. From the saddle where the broad horse path rejoins the trail, you turn south to briefly descend to within 40 yards of noisy, paved Wawona Road, where there is parking for several vehicles. Starting from here cuts 1.9 miles, each way, from the total distance.

Here the Two Hour Ride Trail leaves you, crossing Wawona Road to loop back to the Wawona area. Now on a much less used, generally horse-free route, you climb east up a steepening ridge before veering south up to a usually flowing creek, 1.7 miles beyond the horse trail. The trail maintains its moderate gradient as it next climbs south above the headwalls of two eroding, enlarging bowls. Then in 0.5 mile it begins to switchback up to a broad-crest junction with a ridge trail, about 6.25 miles from the trailhead.

The most direct way from here to the heart of the sequoia grove—its museum—is the following 1.3-mile route. Head 0.8 mile northeast up the Outer Loop Trail to a junction in a fairly level area, branch right and go about 150 yards southeast to cross the grove's tram road, continue 0.2 mile east on another trail, then branch left onto another trail that winds about 250 yards eastward to the museum.

The preferred way is longer, making a 3.7-mile loop. Start south on the Outer Loop Trail, which soon begins a winding, rolling traverse 0.5 mile southwest over to a junction with a northeast-climbing trail, then leads 0.1 mile farther to another junction. Branch left, leaving the Outer Loop Trail, to traverse 0.5 mile to the tunneled California Tree, then in 50 yards reach the famed Grizzly Giant. From it a trail climbs 250 yards north to a crossing of the tram road. This road makes an initial climb southwest to a switchback, from which a minor trail drops southeast, then climbs briefly to a trail paralleling the tram road northwest. You keep to the main trail and make a winding, 400-foot ascent for 0.75 mile to the tram road. From here you'll see the museum, and hiking toward it, you first start north on a trail that quickly reaches a junction, from which you wind about 250 yards eastward to the museum. Complete the loop hike by following the previous paragraph in reverse. There are other trails, some worth taking, some not, but all adding to the distance. These are mentioned in **Day Hike 25**.

DAY HIKE 25
Mariposa Grove of Big Trees

Distance: 6.9 miles loop trip; other routes possible

Grade: 2C, moderate half-day hike

Trailhead: From the Park's south entrance station drive east 2.1 miles up to road's end at the Big Trees parking lot. Be forewarned that by mid-morning it can be full. During summer and early fall, take the free shuttle bus that leaves from the Wawona Store, just northwest of the Wawona Hotel. **C5.**

Near the southwest end of the parking lot is an information kiosk in which visitors can get introduced to the Mariposa Grove while waiting to take the tram. The tram ride gives you an instructive, guided tour of the grove's salient features and, at its stops, you can get off, explore the immediate area, and then get on the next tram. However, by hiking you get a more intimate experience with the giant sequoia and associated plants and animals.

Two trails leave from the eastern, upper end of the parking lot. The northern one is the Outer Loop Trail,

A giant-sequoia cone

which makes a switchbacking climb 0.6 mile north to a junction with a trail east, then a winding traverse 0.6 mile northwest to a junction with a trail down to Wawona (see **Day Hike 24**). Your route is the southern one, which actually starts at the kiosk and runs along the edge of the parking lot. On this nature trail you momentarily parallel the tram road east before crossing a creeklet and the road. The signs along this trail not only identify the notable sequoias, but also educate you on their natural history, including such items as bark, cones, fire, reproduction, and associated plants and animals.

One point worth elaborating is how difficult it is for a sequoia to successfully replace itself. For a seed to become a tree first there must be a fire, which removes humus to expose mineral soil. Then for the seedling to survive, there must be adequate soil moisture. In the last 15 million years, summers generally have been too dry, and almost invariably seedlings died before fall rains arrived. Before then, summers were wetter, especially before 33 million years ago. Today, a seedling is likely to survive only if first there has been a ground fire and then if there has been a heavy snowpack so that the soil will stay moist through the summer. Fortunately, a sequoia can live to 2000+ years in age, producing over a *half billion* seeds in this time, and only one seed is required to replace the parent. The oldest known sequoia—the Muir snag, in the Kings River's Converse Basin Grove—is estimated to have lived for about 3500 years. Sequoias survive because they have "all the time in the world" to wait for proper regenerative conditions.

At the tram-road crossing lies the Fallen Monarch, largely intact, including its roots. Note that they grew in shallow soil, because bedrock lies only a couple of feet down. Unfortunately, occasional severe winds can topple a tree before it reaches old age. From the south side of the road the nature trail climbs 0.25 mile east before crossing the road. At this spot stand the Bachelor and the Three Graces. In a similar distance the trail reaches the Grizzly Giant. Like the Leaning Tower of Pisa, this still-growing

Topographic map of the Mariposa Grove, scale 1:24,000

giant seems ready to fall any second, and one wonders how such a top-heavy, shallow-rooted specimen could have survived as long as it has. Though the largest tree in the Park—and probably the oldest at almost 3,000 years—there are at least 25 specimens elsewhere larger than it. It has a trunk volume of about 34,000 cubic feet, compared to about 52,500 cubic feet for the largest, the General Sherman, in Sequoia National Park's Giant Forest Grove. The Grizzly Giant has enough timber to build about 20 homes, but fortunately sequoia wood is very brittle, shattering when a tree falls—a feature that saved it from being logged into oblivion.

Heading north from the east end of the enclosure circling the Grizzly Giant, you reach in 50 yards the California Tree, also enclosed, but with a path through it. It once had a deep burn, which was cut away in 1895 so that tourists could ride a stage through it. Beyond this tree a trail traverses 0.5 mile west to the Outer Loop Trail. You, however, take an ascending trail that parallels the tram road north for 250 yards before crossing it. The trail then climbs to a nearby switchback from where a lightly used trail winds southeast down to an old road. You start north and quickly reach a lackluster trail that traverses northwest to the tram road, from where another trail, equally lackluster, descends southwest to the Outer Loop Trail. Additionally a switchbacking one climbs northeastward to a loop in the upper part of the tram road.

The trail gains 400 feet elevation climbing to the same spot, starting north and then going briefly east before switchbacking to wind northwest to the upper end of the switchbacking trail, the junction being about 15 yards from the tram road. Here too is the Upper Loop Trail, which parallels the tram road counterclockwise as both circle the upper grove. (Although the area is called the Mariposa Grove, it is really two groves, a lower one from the Grizzly Giant and below, and an upper one encircled by the Upper Loop Trail.)

This guide's suggested route from the junction is to start on a trail a few paces away, which descends north about 90 yards to a junction with an east-west trail (along the most direct way to the Mariposa Grove Museum in **Day Hike 24**). This winds about 250 yards eastward, skirting below restrooms and then passing a west-heading nature trail before reaching the museum, with an adjacent water fountain. In the museum you will find information and displays on the giant sequoia, its related plants and animals, and the area's history. From just east of it you could take a trail 0.3 mile east up to the tram road, beside which you'd spy the lower end of the Fallen Wawona (Tunnel) Tree, which fell during the late winter or spring of 1969. This 2,200-year-old giant, like many others, had a fire-scarred base, and it was enlarged in 1881 for first stagecoaches and much later automobiles to pass through it. An old timer is one who remembers waiting in a long line while each car drove through, stopping to have a

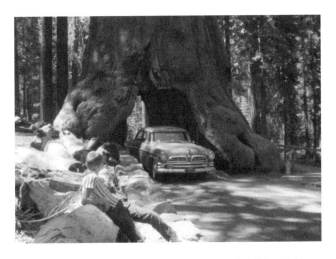

The Fallen Wawona (Tunnel) Tree, before it fell in 1969

passenger get out and photograph the momentous event. Today, the tree is not much to look at.

The suggested route continues from the museum momentarily east along the tram road to a bend. Here is the amazing Telescope Tree, which has been hollowed out by fire. Inside it you can look straight up to the heavens. Despite its great internal loss, this tree is still very much alive, for its vital fluids—as in all trees—are conducted in the sapwood, immediately beneath the thick bark. The heartwood is just dead sapwood whose function is support.

From the back side of the tree you take a trail that climbs 50 yards to the Upper Loop Trail, mentioned earlier. On it you hike 0.3 mile counterclockwise to pass just above the Fallen Wawona Tree, then continue about 250 yards to a crest saddle. Just 40 yards east of it is the Galen Clark Tree, a fine specimen named for the man who first publicized this grove and later became its first guardian. From the saddle a road branches from the tram-road loop, and on it you make an easy climb 0.5 mile to Wawona Point. No sequoias grow along this route, probably because of insufficient ground water. From the point you see the large, partly man-made meadow at Wawona, to the northwest, and the long, curving cliff of Wawona Dome, breaking a sea of green, to the north.

After returning to the crest saddle, you descend west along the Outer Loop Trail, which takes you down almost 3 essentially viewless, sequoia-less miles to the parking lot. The descending trail winds westward about 0.7 mile to a junction. From here a connecting trail goes about 270 yards southeast down to the tram road and the adjacent west end of the nature trail. Onward the Outer Loop Trail descends about 200 yards to a second connecting trail, the one mentioned in **Day Hike 24**, descending about 150 yards southeast to cross the grove's tram road. You continue 0.8 mile southwest on the Outer Loop Trail down to the junction on a broad ridge from where one could follow **Day Hike 24** in reverse 6.25 miles down to Wawona. Instead, you start south on the Outer Loop Trail, which soon begins a winding, rolling traverse 0.5 mile southwest over to a junction with a northeast-climbing trail, then walk 0.1 mile farther to another junction, the eastbound trail from it leading to the California Tree and the Grizzly Giant. Unless you want to make another visit to them (and add about 0.5 mile to your hike) continue southward 0.5 mile down to the parking lot.

Merced Lake

BACKPACK HIKE 1
Merced Lake via Little Yosemite Valley

Distance: 28.2 miles round trip

Grade: 5E, moderate 3-day hike

Trailhead: Just east of the day-use parking lot in Curry Village, drive 0.2 mile southeast along the shuttle-bus road to a short spur road branching right to a backpackers' parking lot. **D1.**

Best done in three days with overnight stops at Little Yosemite Valley and Merced Lake, this hike is often done in two by energetic weekend hikers. Its route up the glaciated Merced River canyon is one of the Sierra's best. Although over half the route lies beyond this guide's area, this popular route is too fine to omit.

See **Day Hike 4** for the first 0.5 mile east to the east bank of the Merced River. **Day Hike 19** describes the route to the Vernal Fall bridge; then you follow the last part of **Day Hike 20** in reverse up the John Muir Trail to Nevada Fall. The last 1.25 miles along this section are very scenic, with views of Half Dome, Mt. Broderick, Liberty Cap, Nevada Fall, and the Merced River canyon. Beyond the Nevada Fall bridge you soon meet the end of the Mist Trail (risky for backpackers), then climb up and over a minor ridge into western Little Yosemite Valley, as described in the second paragraph of **Day Hike 21**.

You leave the northbound John Muir Trail to embark on a shady 2-mile stroll, following the Merced Lake Trail through the broad, flat valley. The valley's floor has been largely buried by glacial sediments, which like beach sand make you work even though the trail is level. Progressing east through Little Yosemite Valley, you stay closer to the base of glacier-polished Moraine Dome than to the Merced River, and along this stretch you can branch off to riverside campsites that are far more peaceful than those near the John Muir Trail junction, which tends to be a "Grand Central Station." The valley's east end is graced by

Supplementary map: the Merced River Trail, scale 1: 62,000

the presence of a beautiful pool—the receptacle of a
Merced River cascade. Leaving the camps of the pictur-
esque area, you climb past the cascade and glance back to
see the east face of exfoliating Moraine Dome.

The brief cascade climb heads toward the 1,900-foot-high, Bunnell Point cliff, which is exfoliating at a prodigious rate. Rounding the base of a glacier-smoothed dome, unofficially called the Sugar Loaf, you enter shady Lost Valley, in which no fires are allowed. At the valley's east end you switchback up past Bunnell Cascade, which with the magnificent canyon scenery can easily distract you from the real danger of this exposed section of trail. Although the scenery may overpower you, past glaciers, which completely buried Bunnell Point, were powerless to effectively erode this part of the canyon. Just beyond, the canyon floor widens a bit, and in this area you bridge the Merced River. The up-canyon walk soon reaches a series of more than a dozen switchbacks that carry you up 400 feet above the river—a bypass route necessitated by another gorge. The climb reaches its zenith amid a spring-fed profuse garden, bordered by aspens, which in midsummer supports a colorful array of various wildflowers.

Beyond this glade you soon come out onto a highly polished bedrock surface. Here you can glance west and see Clouds Rest—a long ridge—standing on the horizon. Now you descend back into tree cover and among the white boles of aspens you brush through a forest carpet of bracken ferns and cross several creeklets before emerging on a bedrock bench above the river's inner gorge. From the bench you can study the features of a broad, hulking granitic mass opposite you whose south face is bounded by an immense arch. A "hairline" crack along its east side indicates that a major rockfall is imminent. Traversing the bench, you soon come to a bend in the river and at it bridge the Merced just above the brink of its cascades. Strolling east, you reach the west end of spacious Echo Valley, and proceed to a junction at its north edge.

Here, near an Echo Creek campsite, is the start of an alternate, less dramatic, high route you could take back to Little Yosemite Valley. But with Merced Lake your goal, you immediately bridge Echo Creek, strike southeast through boggy Echo Valley, and climb east past the

Merced River's largely unseen pools to Merced Lake's west shore. Don't camp here, but rather continue past the north shore to the Merced Lake High Sierra Camp and the adjacent riverside campground, about 9.25 miles beyond the John Muir Trail junction in Little Yosemite Valley. Be sure to use the bearproof storage boxes. Eighty-foot-deep Merced Lake, being a large one at a moderate elevation, supports three species of trout: brook, brown, and rainbow.

BACKPACK HIKE 2
Bridalveil Campground–Wawona Loop

Distance: 30.3 miles semiloop trip

Grade: 5E, moderate 3-day hike

Trailhead: Bridalveil Campground (see Day Hike 13 trailhead). Park at the campground's far end. **C2.**

Sparkling lakes, deep canyons, and alpine crests are *not* found along this hike—but then, neither are the backpacking crowds. This is a hike for those who love quiet trails. Although most of it is forested, you will pass through areas that have been burned in lightning-caused forest fires. The trees are regenerating, and until they cast sufficient shade, shrubs and wildflowers will grow in greater abundance.

From the campground's far end, the trail climbs only about 200 feet in the first 3.3 miles, an excellent way to start a backpack hike. Although white firs and red firs are present, they are greatly overwhelmed by a superabundance of lodgepole pines along this creekside stretch. After about 1.6 miles of it—on a ridge above nearby Bridalveil Creek—you join a trail that comes 1.7 miles from the Glacier Point Road (the **Backpack Hike 3** trailhead). A 1987 fire—one of several in the drainage—caused moderate damage to the forest here. The trail keeps above the creek for a short distance, then curves over to a moderate-size camp along the creek's tributary.

Like others you'll meet, this one can have lots of mosquitoes before late July. A two-minute walk upstream from
the camp ends at the tributary's ford, and on the east bank
you meet the second junction. The lightly used, sometimes obscure trail to the left climbs a short mile east to
the Ostrander Lake Trail (**Backpack Hike 3**).

Turning right, you climb gently south for a mile to the
tributary's upper basin. In it the climb becomes first moderate, and then steep as you struggle briefly up to a nearby
crest that separates the Alder Creek drainage from that of
Bridalveil Creek. Jeffrey pines yield to red firs as you traverse slopes over to a junction near a saddle. The trail
you'll return on climbs east to here from Deer Camp.

Starting southeast, you quickly cross the broad saddle,
enter the Chilnualna Creek drainage, and begin a rolling,
gentle 1.25-mile descent that goes through several small
meadows, all abounding in corn lilies. Just before you
reach the next junction, the trail touches the east edge of
long Turner Meadows, and here you can make a fair
camp.

At the junction you veer right, hop Turner Meadows
creek, then the old trail climbs unnecessarily 300 feet up
to a ridge (originally, horses did the climbing, not hikers,
so ups and downs were not an issue). On this moderate, shady ascent one has a crest view of glaciated-but-
subdued Buena Vista Peak, to the east. You then start a
3,800-foot drop to the Wawona area. On it western white
pines quickly yield to their cousins, the sugar pines, while
farther down red firs yield to the closely related white firs.
A shrubby black oak appears at about 7,540 feet elevation,
near the top of its altitudinal range. This oak is just past a
secondary crest, and from it you plunge down to a creeklet, then make an equally long drop to its larger counter-
part. From its verdant banks you have an easy 0.5-mile
descent to a junction just above Chilnualna Creek. Here,
near the confluence of this creek and its southbound tributary, you can find a suitable spot to spend your first
night. You may want to first view Chilnualna Fall, just
downstream, but be extremely careful if you do, for the

rock can be treacherously slippery and there are no safety railings to keep you from being swept over the fall.

The next day, descend the trail 4.0 scenic miles to its end, following the description of **Day Hike 23** in reverse. Then, gradually descending west, walk 1.3 miles along a road that goes through the private inholding of North Wawona, which has supplies, food, and lodging. Your next trail, the Alder Creek Trail, begins about 0.3 mile beyond the settlement's school, and this trailhead is about 300 yards before the Wawona District Office, which dispenses information and wilderness permits. Before resuming the loop hike, you might consider a side trip to the Pioneer Yosemite History Center, which you enter just west of a junction with the district office's spur road. By walking 200–300 yards upstream from the center's covered bridge you'll discover some small pools in the South Fork Merced River that in summer afternoons are among the warmest "swimming holes" in the Park.

The Alder Creek Trail begins about 100 yards east of a west-heading service road. At this low elevation temperatures often soar into the 80s by early afternoon, and water may be absent until you reach Alder Creek, about 6 miles ahead. After a brief, initial, open climb north, the trail turns west to make an ascending traverse for 0.3 mile across small gullies. At the end of a 2.75-mile-long, mostly viewless ascent, you reach a mile-high junction, from which a steep trail descends 0.75 mile to the heavily traveled Wawona Road.

Starting east, you begin a 2.75-mile rolling traverse in and out of gullies and around or over low ridges to a view of 100-foot-high Alder Creek fall below. Along the last mile or so of this section you may see railroad ties, which are the few tangible relics of a dark period in the Park's history. From the early days of World War I through the 1920s, the Yosemite Lumber Company laid railroad tracks in and around western Park lands to log some of the Sierra's finest stands of sugar pines.

Beyond the fall the abandoned-railroad route approaches lushly lined Alder Creek, parallels it north gently upstream for 1.25 miles, then crosses it to reach a nearby junction. Here or elsewhere along Alder Creek you can make your second night's camp. From the junction a trail climbs north 1.3 miles to an old logging road, on which you could walk 0.5 mile east to the trail's resumption, which for a little over 3 miles first climbs and then barely drops on a direct route to the Bridalveil Campground entrance. Thick brush, however, makes this route undesirable.

The recommended route angles right at the Alder Creek junction, immediately refords the broad creek, and then climbs east for 1.75 miles, paralleling a murmuring tributary. This white-fir-shaded stretch ends at Deer Camp, a desolate roadend flat along the fringe of the former logging area. You can camp here, but it lacks esthetics. Beyond it the trail continues east and, typical of old trails, it winds and switchbacks all too steeply up most of a 1,100-foot ascent. Midway up it, views expand, providing you with an overview of the Alder Creek basin. After about 1.25 miles of climbing, you top a crest, then momentarily descend to a usually flowing creeklet. Should you want to camp in this vicinity, do so at the nearby crest top if mosquitoes are abundant. Leaving the creeklet you climb around a meadow—rich in sedges, willows, and corn lilies—then make a final short push southeast up to a junction near a saddle. From it you retrace your first day's steps 4.9 miles back to the trailhead.

BACKPACK HIKE 3
Glacier Point Road to Ostrander Lake

Distance: 12.7 miles round trip

Grade: 3C, easy 2-day hike

Trailhead: Branch from the Wawona Road and drive 8.9 miles up the Glacier Point Road to a turnoff, on your right. This parking area is 1.3 miles past the Bridalveil Campground spur road. **C2.**

Ostrander Lake, being the closest lake to the Glacier Point Road, is the object of many summertime weekend backpackers. It is also popular in winter and spring with cross-country skiers.

The first half of the hike is easy—a gentle ascent through a forest that is interspersed with an assortment of meadows. You start along a former jeep road, and soon encounter the first of several areas of lodgepole forest badly burned in a 1987 fire. Farther up, on Horizon Ridge, you'll see a forest burned in a 1994 fire. Note the species of new vegetation in these burns. Just 0.3 mile from the trailhead you cross a sluggish creek, then amble an easy mile to a ridge junction. From it a short lateral drops to Bridalveil Creek—possibly a difficult June crossing—then climbs equally briefly to the Bridalveil Creek Trail (**Backpack Hike 2**).

From the junction the route contours southeast past unseen Lost Bear Meadow, and after a mile makes a short ascent east up along a trickling creek to its crossing. Just beyond the ford the road curves west to a nearby junction with a second lateral to the Bridalveil Creek Trail. Though you are now about halfway to Ostrander Lake, you've climbed very little, and from this junction you face 1,500 feet of vertical gain, mostly through burned forests. Nevertheless, some trees survived, and they indicate the former (and future) forest type.

The steepening road climbs east through a mixed forest, then climbs more gently south across an open slab that provides the first views of the Bridalveil Creek basin. You then curve southeast into a Jeffrey-pine stand, then climb east through a white-fir forest. These firs are largely supplanted by red firs by the time you top a saddle that bisects Horizon Ridge. Climbing southeast up that ridge, the road passes through an open stretch that supports an eastern Sierra species—sagebrush. About 400 feet above the first saddle the road switchbacks at a second one, then curves up to a third. From it the road makes a momentary descent southeast before bending to start a short, final ascent south into unburned forest surrounding Ostrander Lake. Near this bend you get far-ranging views across the Illilouette Creek basin. You can see the tops of Royal Arches and Washington Column and, above and east of them, see North, Basket, and Half domes. Behind Half Dome stands the Park's geographic center, broad-topped Mt. Hoffmann. Reigning over the Illilouette Creek basin is Mt. Starr King and its entourage of lesser domes. To the east and northeast the jagged crest of the Clark Range cuts the sky.

Beyond the short, final ascent south you drop in several minutes to Ostrander Hut. When it is snowbound, cross-country skiers can stay in it, if they've first obtained reservations from the Park's Wilderness Center (see "The Trails," p. 17). The hut is on a rocky glacial moraine left by a small glacier that retreated perhaps 16,000 years ago. Behind it, lying in a bedrock basin, is 25-acre, trout-populated Ostrander Lake. Here, camping is good along the west shore.

Experienced hikers can head cross-country southeast 0.25 mile to a pond, then east over a ridge to a shallow bowl holding the Hart Lakes. The larger one has a rather stark granitic backdrop, the glacier-smoothed northeast face of Horse Ridge. After perhaps camping nearby, you can then descend northeast to the Buena Vista Trail, hopefully meeting it atop the crest of a sizable moraine. (If you're too low, you may end up at Edson Lake.) Either head down the Buena Vista Trail and then west out the Mono Meadow Trail, for a 19.6-mile loop trip (with a short vehicle shuttle), or else head up the Buena Vista Trail for more lake hunting, described in the next hike.

BACKPACK HIKE 4
Mono Meadow to Buena Vista and Royal Arch Lakes

Distance: 30.4 miles round trip

Grade: 5E, easy 4-day hike

Trailhead: Branch from the Wawona Road and drive 10.1 miles up the Glacier Point Road to a forested saddle with a parking area, on your right. **D2.**

The subalpine lakes nestled around Buena Vista Peak can be reached from North Wawona—Backpack Hike 5—or from three trailheads along the Glacier Point Road. This hike starts from one of these trailheads and visits five of the area's lakes. Although this route is slightly longer than Backpack Hike 5, it requires 20% less climbing effort.

Starting in a stand of red firs, the trail begins with a steady, moderate descent north, followed by an easing gradient east to lodgepole-fringed Mono Meadow. Until mid-July you may face 200 yards of muddy freshets and meadow bogs before you reach the narrow meadow's east edge. During this period, desperate hikers try to circumvent the mire, and several paths may spring up to confuse you. The real trail crosses the meadow on a 120° bearing, and it becomes obvious once you're within the forest's edge.

Beyond the meadow the Mono Meadow Trail crosses a low divide, then makes a generally viewless, easy descent to a major tributary of Illilouette Creek. Here, 1.5 miles from the trailhead, is the first possible campsite. You ford the tributary at the brink of some rapids, and in early season this ford could be a dangerous one. From the tributary you have a short though unnecessary climb, with 200 feet of elevation gain. The climb does have some merit,

for at the crest and on the descent east from it you're rewarded with views of North, Basket, and Half domes,
Clouds Rest, and Mt. Starr King. After a descent through a
fir forest you emerge on an open slope and descend
straight toward Mt. Starr King, the highest of the Illilouette Creek domes.

Immediately after the view disappears, you reach a
junction with the Buena Vista Trail, which links Glacier
Point with the Buena Vista Peak area. Turning right, you
go 40 yards up-canyon to a second junction, from where
the Mono Meadow Trail goes 300 yards east past campsites to ford broad Illilouette Creek. From it the trail
climbs a slope veneered with glacial outwash—stream deposits from the last glaciers that lay up-canyon—then it
crosses a bedrock bench with a veneer of gravel. In the
"classic" U.S. Geological Survey Professional Paper 160 on
Yosemite Valley, this gravel was considered to be sediments of a hypothetical glacial lake, which supposedly existed hundreds of thousands of years ago. Actually the
gravel, as elsewhere in the Sierra, is nothing more than
weathered granitic bedrock. This is also true of gravel on
benches in this drainage, which incorrectly were called
glacial deposits. Of more interest to the hiker is that this
spacious bedrock bench is suitable for camping. On it a
trail climbs east to a junction near two interesting domes.
Two rather mediocre Merced Pass Lakes, lying east beyond the area, by themselves are not worth the 12.75-mile
hike from the trailhead to reach them.

From the junction before the creek crossing you climb
southeast up the Buena Vista Trail. Over much of the
route up toward Buena Vista Peak the vegetation has been
burned by several large, natural fires. Usually a burn is
quite unsightly for a year or two, but wildflowers often
abound in one, and after several years brush and young
trees soften the visual effect. In 1.25 miles you come to a
creeklet with a fair camp on its west bank. The trail's gradient gradually eases, then you cross a broad divide and in
0.25 mile angle sharply left to descend along the edge of a
sloping meadow. Beyond it you encounter aspens that

**Half Dome and Mt. Starr King, from
slabs above Edson Lake**

hide a step-across creek. Just a few minutes' walk east of it
you cross a slightly larger creek, then make a gentle ascent
southeast across sandy soils to steep slopes above Buena
Vista Creek. Camping is poor along the west bank, but
good—and isolated—above the east bank. Fallen trees
may provide access across the bouldery creek to these
sites.

Soon the trail leaves Buena Vista Creek, curves southwest and climbs moderately in that direction for 1.5 miles
to a ford, between two meadows, of diminutive Edson
Lake creek. From a poor campsite the trail ascends along
a moraine crest, then in one mile leaves it to angle southeast up to a higher crest. Where the trail makes this sudden angle left, you can leave it and contour 0.3 mile west
over to a campsite at shallow Edson Lake. The trail follows the higher moraine crest southwest for more than
300 yards, finally leaves the burned area, and then makes a

0.25-mile, view-packed descent to Hart Lakes creek. From where the trail leaves the crest, you can continue cross-country southwest up it, soon diagonal up slabs, then climb south up to the Hart Lakes.

From brush-lined Hart Lakes creek you make a short contour over to Buena Vista Creek, having a small camp-site on its east bank. After 0.5 mile of moderate ascent you cross a creek that bends northeast, then continue south up a slightly shorter ascent to a recrossing of that creek. Immediately beyond you cross its western tributary, then follow this stream south briefly up to two ponds, from which you switchback up a cirque wall with ice-shattered blocks to a crest junction. **Backpack Hike 5**, ascending from North Wawona, now joins the route for a loop around the lakes of Buena Vista Peak. The first lake you encounter, about 0.3 mile southeast from the junction, is rather bleak Buena Vista Lake, which has rainbow and brook trout. Nestled on a broad bench at the base of the cool north slope of Buena Vista Peak, this lake is the high-est and coldest one you'll see. It does, however, have two good camps.

Starting at the lake's outlet, you ascend short switch-backs up to a broad pass. From the viewless pass you can climb 0.75 mile up a gentle ridge to Buena Vista Peak for an unrestricted panorama of the Park's southern area. Peak baggers take note: at 9,709 feet elevation, this sum-mit is the highest one in the *Yosemite* 15′ quadrangle. From the pass you descend 2 easy, winding trail miles to a favorite lake on this loop, Royal Arch Lake, which lies below a broad, granitic arch. This lake, like Buena Vista Lake, has rainbow and brook trout. Just past the outlet, near the lake's southwest corner, is an excellent, though often occupied, campsite. For more solitude you can head cross-country 0.75 mile west to less attractive Minnow Lake, which has brook trout.

Leaving Royal Arch Lake, you parallel its outlet creek for 0.5 mile, then angle south across slabs to a junc-tion with a trail that goes first to Buck Camp (a ranger station) and then to Chiquito Pass. From the junction

Royal Arch Lake

you descend west toward Johnson Lake, reaching good campsites along its northwest shore in just 0.75 mile—with hordes of mosquitoes in early season. You don't see large Crescent Lake, but on meeting its inlet creek, about 0.3 mile beyond a meadowy divide, one can walk 150 yards downstream, passing a fair camp before reaching the lake's shallow, trout-filled waters. You might visit or camp near the lake's south end, for from its outlet you can peer into the 2,800-foot-deep South Fork Merced River canyon.

Beyond Crescent Lake's inlet creek the trail quickly turns north, passes a small creekside meadow, and then climbs more than 150 feet to a second broad divide. From it you descend into the headwaters of a Chilnualna Creek tributary. The moderate-to-steep gradient ends when you approach easily missed Grouse Lake. Look for a use trail that descends about 100 yards to a fair campsite on the north shore of this shallow, reedy lakelet.

Lodgepoles and red firs monopolize the slopes along the 2-mile descent from this lake down to a hillside junction. From here, hikers completing **Backpack Hike 5** head west down-canyon to their trailhead. Hikers on the second day of that hike join you for a short northwest stretch, first up over a nearby divide, then down more than 400 feet to Chilnualna Creek. Just above its north bank is a good, medium-size campsite, and just beyond that is another trail junction. From it **Backpack Hike 5** trekkers climb east. Should you want to visit the Chilnualna Lakes, take this 5.3-mile trail up past them to the crest junction where **Backpack Hike 5** first joined the route, then backtrack 13.1 miles to the trailhead. This route is 10.0 miles longer than the following route, including its 1.2-mile walk along the Glacier Point Road back to the trailhead.

Spurning the longer option, you head northwest from Chilnualna Creek. During midsummer, the gently ascending traverse is brightened by the orange sunbursts of alpine lilies, growing chest-high along the wetter parts of the trail. As you near Turner Meadows you encounter a trail junction from which **Backpack Hike 2** departs southwest down to the Wawona area.

You now backtrack along the first part of that hike, first ascending past and through a series of "Turner Meadows," then topping a forest pass to quickly meet a trail descending to Deer Camp. You, however, keep right, traverse to a crest and descend to a tributary of Bridalveil Creek. But before reaching Bridalveil Creek, you meet a junction, turn left and then cross the tributary creek. Along it you momentarily pass a moderate-size campsite and then in 0.5 mile reach another junction. The main trail continues 1.6 miles northwest to Bridalveil Campground, but you veer right, drop to nearby Bridalveil Creek, ford it, and make an equally short climb up to the Ostrander Lake Trail—a closed jeep road. In 1.5 miles the northbound route ends at the Glacier Point Road, beside which you walk 1.2 miles east to the trailhead.

God bless Yosemite bears!

— John Muir

BACKPACK HIKE 5
North Wawona to Royal Arch, Buena Vista, and Chilnualna Lakes

Distance: 28.3 miles semiloop trip

Grade: 5E, easy 4-day hike

Trailhead: Same as the Day Hike 23 trailhead. **C5.**

Glaciers originating on the slopes of Buena Vista Peak descended north, south, and west, then retreated to leave about a dozen small-to-medium-size lakes. This hike visits seven of these plus dashing Chilnualna Fall—one of the Park's highest falls outside Yosemite Valley.

Day Hike 23 guides you up through a changing forest to campsites—a possible first night's stop—in an area around a trail junction near a south-flowing tributary of Chilnualna Creek. From that tributary the trail makes a short, steep ascent northeast, then traverses southeast. Soon reaching Chilnualna Creek, you'll find additional campsites along both its banks.

After crossing to the southeast bank, you head upstream, then veer away from the creek to make a short, moderate ascent to a low gap. Past it you enter a damp meadow—an early-season mosquito haven—then climb for a mile, paralleling the usually unseen creek at a distance before you intersect its tributary, Grouse Lake creek. Generally a jump-across creek, it can be a 20-foot wide, slippery-slab ford in June. Now just above 7,000 feet, you feel the effects of a higher elevation as well as see them— as expressed in the predominance of stately red firs and occasional lodgepole pines. Before reaching a junction after a 0.75-mile ascent, you also note the first trailside western white pines.

At the junction you join **Backpack Hike 4** for a short northwest stretch, first up over a nearby divide, then down more than 400 feet to Chilnualna Creek. Just above its north bank is a good, medium-size campsite, and just beyond that is another trail junction. Here you turn right while **Backpack Hike 4** continues ahead, bound for Turner Meadows and the Glacier Point Road.

Eastbound, you make a moderate 0.25-mile ascent, followed by a gentler one that goes 1.25 miles along the lodgepole-shaded bank of Chilnualna Creek. After a 0.25-mile walk along this gentler stretch, you'll find an acceptable campsite. At the end of the stretch you cross the seasonal creek that drains the middle and northern Chilnualna Lakes. You go a few yards along the larger creek that drains the southern and eastern Chilnualna Lakes, then leave it to cross a nearby bouldery ridge of a glacial moraine.

Young glacial evidence in the form of moraines, erratics, and polish is often seen along the remaining 1.6-mile, shady climb to the waist-deep southern Chilnualna Lake. Being so shallow, it is one this route's warmest lakes for cooling off in. The best of the Chilnualna Lakes is also the least visited: the lake at the base of Buena Vista Peak's western shoulder, about 0.5 mile east-southeast of the trailside lake. A more-frequented lake is the middle one, which is easier to reach. From the far end of the southern lake, head 0.25 mile up its inlet creek to a small pond, then walk due north over a low ridge to the middle lake. From it one can easily regain the trail by continuing north—no need to drop along its outlet creek.

Leaving the trailside southern lake and its fair west-shore campsite, you climb over a low, bouldery morainal ridge, skirt a small meadow, and cross the middle lake's ephemeral creek. Past it you curve over to the northern lake's outlet creek, parallel it upward, and then, just 0.25 mile before the lake, cross over to the north bank. Upon reaching the shallow, narrow lake you find a good campsite among red firs and western white pines. If weather is threatening, camp here rather than climb east to the exposed pass.

At that 9,040-foot-high pass, about a 0.75-mile winding ascent from the northern lake, you meet the Buena Vista Trail. Now you follow most of the second half of **Backpack Hike 4** as it goes past Buena Vista, Royal Arch,

Johnson, Crescent, and Grouse lakes. You may want to visit all of them, and you should plan to spend at least a day in this scenic glacier-lake area. A little more than 2 miles west of Grouse Lake you'll leave **Backpack Hike 4** where you first met it, and descend the way you came—past Chilnualna Fall.

Recommended Reading

Arce, Gary. 1996. *Defying Gravity: High Adventure on Yosemite's Walls.* Berkeley: Wilderness Press, 194 p.

Aune, Philip S., technical coordinator. 1994. *Proceedings of the Symposium on Giant Sequoias: Their Place in the Ecosystem and Society.* Albany, CA: U.S. Forest Service Pacific Southwest Research Station, 170 p.

Beck, Steve. 1995. *Yosemite Trout Fishing Guide.* Portland, OR: Amato Publications, 158 p.

Botti, Stephen J., and Walter Sydoriak. 2001. *An Illustrated Flora of Yosemite National Park.* El Portal, CA: Yosemite Association, 484 p.

Calkins, Frank C., N. King Huber, and Julie A. Roller. 1985. *Bedrock Geologic Map of Yosemite Valley, Yosemite National Park, California.* Washington: U.S. Geological Survey, Map I-1639.

Gaines, David. 1992. *Birds of Yosemite and the East Slope.* Lee Vining, CA: Artemisia Press, 352 p.

Gibbens, Robert P., and Harold F. Heady. 1964. *The Influence of Modern Man on the Vegetation of Yosemite Valley.* Berkeley: Univ. of Calif. Div. of Agricultural Sciences, Manual 36, 44 p.

Grater, Russell K., and Tom A. Blaue. 1978. *Discovering Sierra Mammals.* El Portal, CA: Yosemite Association, 174 p.

Hickman, James C., editor. 1993. *The Jepson Manual: Higher Plants of California.* Berkeley: University of California Press, 1400 p.

Horn, Elizabeth L. 1998. *Sierra Nevada Wildflowers.* Missoula, MT: Mountain Press, 215 p.

Niehaus, Theodore F., and Charles L. Ripper. 1981. *A Field Guide to Pacific States Wildflowers.* Boston: Houghton Mifflin Company, 432 p.

Russell, Carl P. 1992. *One Hundred Years in Yosemite.* El Portal, CA: Yosemite Association, 268 p.

Schaffer, Jeffrey P. 1999. *Yosemite National Park: A Natural-History Guide to Yosemite and Its Trails.* Berkeley: Wilderness Press, 274 p.

Schaffer, Jeffrey P. 1997. *The Geomorphic Evolution of the Yosemite Valley and Sierra Nevada Landscapes: Solving the Riddles in the Rocks.* Berkeley: Wilderness Press, 388 p.

Sibley, David A. 2000. *The Sibley Guide to Birds.* New York: Alfred A. Knopf, 544 p.

Stuart, John D., and John O. Sawyer. 2001. *Trees and Shrubs of California.* Berkeley: University of California Press, 467 p.

Weeden, Norman F. 1996. *A Sierra Nevada Flora.* Berkeley: Wilderness Press, 259 p.

Willard, Dwight. 2000. *A Guide to the Sequoia Groves of California.* El Portal, CA: Yosemite Association, 124 p.

Winnett, Thomas, and Melanie Findling. 1994. *Backpacking Basics.* Berkeley: Wilderness Press, 134 p.

Index